Dizzy Gillespie

THE BEBOP YEARS 1937–1952
KEN VAIL

The Scarecrow Press, Inc.
Lanham, Maryland, and Oxford
2003

SCARECROW PRESS, INC.

Published in the United States of America
by Scarecrow Press, Inc.
A wholly owned subsidary of
The Rowman & Littlefield Publishing Group, Inc.
4501 Forbes Boulevard, Suite 200, Lanham, Maryland 20706
www.scarecrowpress.com

PO Box 317
Oxford
OX2 9RU, UK

British Library Cataloguing in Publication Information Available

Library of Congress Cataloging-in-Publication Data Available

0-8108-4880-5 (pbk.: alk. paper)

♾TM The paper used in this publication meets the minimum
requirements of American National Standard for Information
Sciences—Permanence of Paper for Printed Library Materials,
ANSI/NISO Z39.48-1992.
Manufactured in the United States of America.

Acknowledgements
My grateful thanks to:
My wife, Marian, and my children, Sam and Emily;
Rolf Dahlgren for his generosity in sharing his photographs;
Down Beat and *Metronome* magazines;
Ron Fritts for his research collection of itinerary dates and
advertisements;
Jimmy Heath for sharing his photographs and his recollections;
Franz Hoffmann for his amazing series of books, *Jazz Advertised*;
Wolfram Knauer of the Jazz-Institut Darmstadt;
David Nathan of the National Jazz Foundation Archive at
Loughton;
Brian Peerless for sharing his collection of *Metronomes* and *Down
Beats* and much more besides;
Alyn Shipton for sharing some of his research for his award-
winning book *Groovin' High*;
Tony Shoppee for sharing his *Down Beat* collection;

I would also like to acknowledge the kind assistance of
Dick Bank, Lorraine Gillespie, Milt Hinton, Bob Inman, Charles
'The Whale' Lake, Stan Levey, Jan Mulder, Dieter Salemann,
Duncan Schiedt, Don Tarrant, Peter Vacher, Theo Zwicky.

I have also been grateful for the writings of W. Bruynincx, Leonard
Feather, Gary Giddins, Ralph Gleason, Nat Hentoff, Jorgen Grunnet
Jepsen, Gene Lees, Mike Levin, Alun Morgan, Robert Reisner, Ross
Russell, Phil Schaap, Barry Ulanov.

Photographs from the collections of Rolf Dahlgren, Brian Foskett,
Jimmy Heath, Duncan Schiedt, and the author.

Preface

The Jazz Itineraries set out to provide a fascinating insight into the life and times of some of my favourite jazz musicians, in this case... Dizzy Gillespie. Using contemporary photographs, newspaper reports, advertisements and reviews, I have attempted to chronicle his life through the birth of bebop, the demise of his first big band, up to his departure for France in 1952. I have tried to include all known club, concert, television, film and jam session appearances as well as his recordings, although this is not intended to be a discography.

I hope that you will find this book an informative accompaniment when listening to Dizzy's records or reading any of his biographies.

Ken Vail, Cambridge, August 2000

Sunday 21 October 1917
John Birks Gillespie is born in Cheraw, South Carolina. He is the last of nine children born to Lottie and James Gillespie.

1922
John Birks begins school at the Robert Smalls Public School.

Above: John Birks Gillespie (right) with his older brother Wesley.

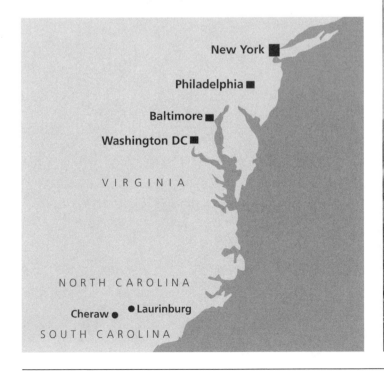

June 1927
John Birks Gillespie's father dies from an asthma attack.

1929
John Birks takes an interest in the musical shows put on by his teacher Alice Wilson. When the school acquires some instruments, John Birks volunteers for the school band and is given a trombone. He practises hard,but realises that trombone is not the instrument for him. At Christmas, neighbour Brother Harrington is given atrumpet. John Birks falls in love with it, spending all his time at the neighbours house practising the trumpet.

1930
John Birks and a few of his school friends form a little band and play at local dances.

1933
Dizzy graduates from Robert Smalls and after a summer digging ditches goes to the Laurinburg Technical Institute in Laurinburg, North Carolina on a scholarship.

1934
John Birks enjoys the atmosphere at Laurinburg and begins to take music seriously, practicing and studying constantly. He teaches himself to read and learns some theory.

Spring 1935

Mrs Gillespie and her family leave North Carolina to live in Philadelphia. Dizzy, aged 17, stays to finish high school at Laurinburg but flunks physics and leaves without graduating. He travels north to Philadelphia and joins his mother, sister Mattie and her husband, sister Eugenia, and brother Wesley and his wife in an apartment at 637 Pine Street. Mattie's husband, Bill, is friendly toward John Birks and buys him a trumpet from Harry's Pawnshop. John Birks carries the trumpet around in a paper bag, joins the union, and soon gets a job in the Frankie Fairfax Band and it is around this time that he acquires the nickname of Dizzy.

Above: Dizzy kneels (second from right, front row) next to bandleader Frankie Fairfax.

1936

When Frankie Fairfax reorganises his band, Dizzy finds himself in a trumpet section with Charlie Shavers and Carl 'Bama' Warwick. Shavers is a Roy Eldridge fan, like Dizzy, and knows all of Roy's solos. The trio become very friendly but when Tiny Bradshaw comes to town to recruit a trumpet section to play the Astoria Ballroom in Baltimore, Shavers and Warwick are unable to persude Dizzy to leave home.

1937

Charlie Shavers and Bama Warwick join the Lucky Millinder Band and try to get Dizzy into the band. Dizzy goes to New York and stays with his brother, J.P. on 142nd Street between Sevent and Eighth Avenue. The job with Lucky Millinder falls through, but Dizzy decides to stay and rough it out in New York. He hangs out at the Savoy Ballroom on Lenox Avenue, sitting in at every opportunity with the Savoy Sultans, Willie Bryant, Fess Williams, Claude Hopkins, Teddy Hill and Chick Webb.

One night in May, Dizzy meets up with Teddy Hill at the Savoy. Teddy Hill is about to go to Europe and his second trumpeter, Frankie Newton, doesn't want to make the trip. Dizzy volunteers and joins the Teddy Hill Band.

Monday 17 May 1937

Dizzy Gillespie records with the Teddy Hill Band for Bluebird in New York City.

TEDDY HILL (tenor sax/director); BILL DILLARD (trumpet/vocal); SHAD COLLINS, DIZZY GILLESPIE (trumpets); DICKIE WELLS (trombone); RUSSELL PROCOPE (clarinet/alto sax); HOWARD JOHNSON (alto sax); ROBERT CARROLL (tenor sax); SAM ALLEN (piano); JOHN SMITH (guitar); RICHARD FULLBRIGHT (bass); BILL BEASON (drums)

San Anton' (vBD) / *I'm Happy, Darling, Dancing With You* / *Yours And Mine* (vBD) / *I'm Feeling Like A Million* (vBD) / *King Porter Stomp* / *Blue Rhythm Fantasy*

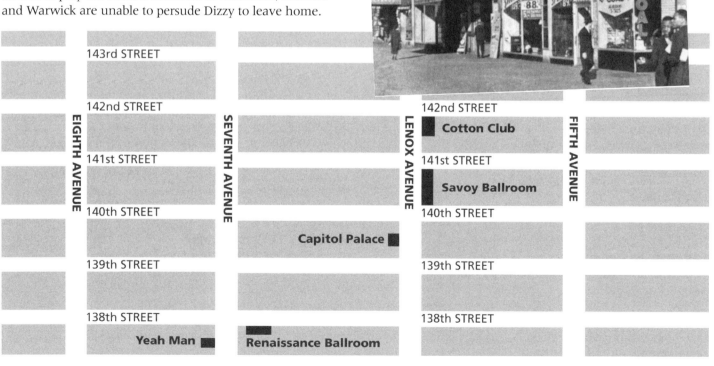

143rd STREET

142nd STREET

EIGHTH AVENUE

SEVENTH AVENUE

141st STREET

140th STREET

Capitol Palace

139th STREET

138th STREET

Yeah Man

Renaissance Ballroom

142nd STREET

LENOX AVENUE

FIFTH AVENUE

Cotton Club

141st STREET

Savoy Ballroom

140th STREET

139th STREET

138th STREET

late May 1937

Dizzy Gillespie, the Teddy Hill Band and the Cotton Club Show set sail for Europe aboard the *Ile de France*.

Saturday 29 May 1937

The English *Melody Maker* reports:

Teddy Hill en route for Paris—or perhaps there by now.

June 1937

Dizzy Gillespie and the Teddy Hill Band open at the Ambassador Theatre in Paris. While there, a row breaks out when a pirate radio attempts to broadcast secretly from the theatre. The *Melody Maker* is outraged:

COTTON CLUB SHOW VICTIMS OF ATTEMPTED RADIO PIRACY IN PARIS

Dizzy Gillespie, the Teddy Hill Band and the Cotton Club Show move on to the Moulin Rouge in Paris, where the show is reviewed by Leonard Feather for the 10th July edition of the *Melody Maker*:

Bill Dillard, John Gillespie, Lester 'Shad' Collins (trumpets); Dickie Wells, Wilbur de Paris (trombones); Teddy Hill (clarinet, alto sax); Howard Johnson (clarinet, alto sax); Russell Procope (clarinet, alto sax); Robert Carroll (tenor sax); Sam Allen (piano); John Smith Jr. (guitar); Dick Fulbright (bass); William Beason (drums).

This band, with the whole superb Cotton Club revue at the Moulin Rouge, defies any brief description.

For the present, let it be said that no greater band, except Ellington's, has ever come to Europe; and that when he opens at the Palladium on July 26, the first U.S. band to work here for several years, there will be little or no dissension concerning its brilliance.

Monday 26 July 1937

Dizzy Gillespie, the Teddy Hill Band and the Cotton Club Show open a five-week season at the London Palladium in England. Dizzy jams after-hours at the Nest Club. During the day he roams the city, and buys a green tweed coat that is to cause a sensation when he shows it off in Harlem.

Saturday 28 August 1937

Dizzy Gillespie, the Teddy Hill Band and the Cotton Club Show close at the London Palladium.

The band also play two weeks at the Royal Theatre in Dublin and two weeks at the Palace Theatre in Manchester before sailing for home on 14 September.

Dizzy proudly poses on a London street to show of his brand new green tweed coat.

When Dizzy returns he finds that he can't work with the band in New York until he completes a 3-month waiting period to join Local 802. The union allows him to take single gigs, however, and he plays some jobs with Cass Carr, a West Indian bass player who doubles on musical saw. Dizzy also works occasionally with the Edgar Hayes Band and on one occasion, without union permission, plays a weekend gig with them in Washington, D.C. Here he meets Lorraine Willis, a young dancer who is working on the T.O.B.A. circuit between Washington, Baltimore, Philadelphia and the Apollo Theatre in Harlem. Dizzy is very attracted by Lorraine but she is cool towards him.

Thursday 21 October 1937

Dizzy Gillespie's 20th birthday.

Without warning, Dizzy's brother J.P. moves out of the apartment they share on 139th Street, Dizzy finds life very hard. Work is very scarce for him and he hangs out at the Apollo on the chance of seeing Lorraine. She takes pity on him and makes sure that he has enough money to eat.

1938

When Dizzy's probation period is up, he gets his union card and rejoins the Teddy Hill Band. Bob Inman (then a jazz-mad teenager) remembers seeing Dizzy with Teddy Hill's Band at the Savoy Ballroom on Saturday 8th January, alternating with the Willie Bryant Band. Dizzy takes most of the hot trumpet choruses and later signs an autograph for Bob.

Best Wishes.
Sincerely,
John (Diz) Gillespie

Whenever Teddy Hill isn't working, Dizzy plays with Edgar Hayes, Alberto Socarras and the Savoy Sultans. Al Cooper's Savoy Sultans are resident at the Savoy Ballroom, but whenever they have a date at the Apollo Theatre they add a third trumpet player, usually Dizzy.

Friday 15 July 1938
Dizzy Gillespie joins the Edgar Hayes Band for a one-week engagement at the Apollo Theatre in New York City. Dizzy meets drummer Kenny Clarke for the first time.

Thursday 21 July 1938
Dizzy Gillespie and the Edgar Hayes Band close at the Apollo Theatre in New York City.

For the next year, Dizzy does pretty well, gigging with Teddy Hill, Edgar Hayes, Alberto Socarras and the Savoy Sultans, and seeing Lorraine whenever he can. He also gets Kenny Clarke into the Teddy Hill Band. Dizzy is beginning to formulate his ideas and he likes the way Kenny sounds behind him, breaking up the time and dropping 'bombs.'

Friday 21 October 1938
Dizzy Gillespie's 21st birthday.

Thursday 30 March 1939

Dizzy and the Teddy Hill Band play a one-nighter at the State Armory in Greenwich, Connecticut.

Friday 31 March 1939

Dizzy and the Teddy Hill Band open a one-week engagement at the Apollo Theatre in New York City. Also on the bill are the 3 Dandridge Sisters and Tip, Tap & Toe.

Thursday 6 April 1939

Dizzy and the Teddy Hill Band close at the Apollo Theatre in New York City.

Saturday 15 April 1939

Dizzy and the Teddy Hill Band play a charity dance at the Rockland Palace in New York City. The Teddy Wilson Band share the bill.

June 1939

Dizzy and the Teddy Hill Band open at the World's Fair in Flushing, New York, playing in the reconstruction of the Savoy Ballroom.

New York World's Fair has a replica of Harlem's Savoy ballroom with Teddy Hill's band playing for lindy hoppers and the like…Spot right now is about the fair's biggest attraction, as far as dance bands go.

THAT WAS SOME WEIRD SHIT. THEY BUILT A SAVOY BALLROOM, A PAVILION, OUT IN THE WORLD'S FAIR FOR A "LINDY HOPPER SHOW." THEY USED TEDDY HILL'S BAND; NO DANCING WAS ALLOWED, JUST A SHOW. IT WAS OUT IN FLUSHING MEADOWS. THEN WE GOT INTO A DISPUTE WITH THE UNION…MOE GALE AND SAM SUBER WERE RELATED IN SOME WAY. MOE GALE WAS THE OWNER OF THE SAVOY BALLROOM, AND SAM SUBER WAS AN OFFICIAL OF THE UNION. THEY GOT IN CAHOOTS AND MADE THE PAY SCALE AT THE WORLD'S FAIR THIRD-CLASS SCALE, INSTEAD OF FIRST-CLASS, WHICH IT SHOULD HAVE BEEN. WE WERE DOING ABOUT "EIGHTY" SHOWS A DAY; ON-OFF, ON-OFF, ON-OFF, SO THE WHOLE BAND, ALL OF US, WENT DOWN TO THE UNION TO PROTEST AGAINST THIS.
SO BECAUSE TEDDY HILL WENT TO THE UNION, THEY FIRED TEDDY'S WHOLE BAND.

Friday 11 August 1939
Dizzy and the Teddy Hill Band open a one-week engagement at the Apollo Theatre in New York City. Also on the bill are the Boogie Woogie Boys, Billie Holiday, Pigmeat Markham and Tip, Tap & Toe.

While at the Apollo, Dizzy tries out with the Cab Calloway Band at the Cotton Club. He gets the job:

> RUDOLPH [CAB CALLOWAY'S VALET] CALLED ME WHEN I WAS AT THE APOLLO WORKING WITH TEDDY HILL AND SAID, "COME ON DOWN HERE."
> I HAD NEVER SPOKEN TO CAB, SO I ASKED HIM, "SHOULD I BRING MY HORN?"
> "YEAH, YEAH. YOU START TONIGHT."
> I WENT DOWNTOWN TO THE COTTON CLUB, PUT ON A UNIFORM AND BLEW, DIDN'T EVEN ASK WHAT SALARY CAB WAS PAYING.

Below: The Teddy Hill band on stage at the Apollo. Dizzy is third from left in the trumpet section. The drummer is Kenny Clarke.

Thursday 17 August 1939
Dizzy and the Teddy Hill Band close at the Apollo Theatre in New York City.

Dizzy joins the Cab Calloway Band at the Cotton Club at 48th and Broadway. Dizzy and bassist Milt Hinton spend intermissions on the roof, where Dizzy teaches him new chord substitutions and harmonies.

Wednesday 30 August 1939
Dizzy records with the Cab Calloway Band in New York. CAB CALLOWAY (vocal); DIZZY GILLESPIE, MARIO BAUZA, LAMAR WRIGHT (trumpets); CLAUDE JONES, KEG JOHNSON, DEPRIEST WHEELER (trombones); CHAUNCEY HAUGHTON, ANDREW BROWN (clarinet/alto sax); CHU BERRY, WALTER THOMAS (tenor sax); BENNY PAYNE (piano); DANNY BARKER (guitar); MILT HINTON (bass); COZY COLE (drums)
For The Last Time I Cried Over You (vCC) / *Twee-Twee-Tweet* (vCC) / *Pluckin' The Bass* / *I Ain't Gettin' Nowhere Fast* (vCC)

Monday 11 September 1939
Dizzy records with Lionel Hampton and his orchestra. DIZZY GILLESPIE (trumpet); BENNY CARTER (alto sax); COLEMAN HAWKINS, BEN WEBSTER, CHU BERRY (tenor sax); CLYDE HART (piano); CHARLIE CHRISTIAN (guitar); MILT HINTON (bass); COZY COLE (drums); LIONEL HAMPTON (vibes/vocal)
When Lights Are Low (2 takes) / *One Sweet Letter From You* (vLH) / *Hot Mallets* / *Early Session Hop*

Saturday 23 September 1939
Dizzy and the Cab Calloway Band close at the Cotton Club in New York City.

Monday 25 September 1939
Dizzy and the Cab Calloway Band open a one-week engagement at the Palace Theatre in Hartford, Connecticut.

Saturday 30 September 1939
Dizzy and the Cab Calloway Band close at the Palace Theatre in Hartford, Connecticut.

Thursday 5 October 1939
Dizzy and the Cab Calloway Band open a one-week engagement at the Windsor Theatre in the Bronx, New York City.

Wednesday 11 October 1939
Dizzy and the Cab Calloway Band close at the Windsor Theatre in the Bronx, New York City.

Thursday 12 October 1939
Dizzy and the Cab Calloway Band open a one-week engagement at the Audubon Theatre, 165th Street and Broadway, New York City.

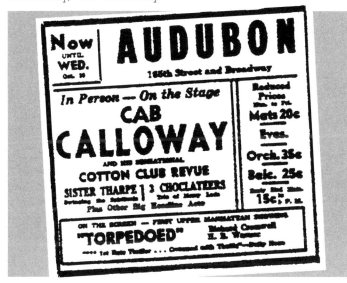

Tuesday 17 October 1939
Dizzy records with the Cab Calloway Band in New York City.
CAB CALLOWAY (vocal); DIZZY GILLESPIE, MARIO BAUZA, LAMAR WRIGHT (trumpets); CLAUDE JONES, KEG JOHNSON, DEPRIEST WHEELER (trombones); CHAUNCEY HAUGHTON, ANDREW BROWN (clarinet/alto sax); CHU BERRY, WALTER THOMAS (tenor sax); BENNY PAYNE (piano); DANNY BARKER (guitar); MILT HINTON (bass); COZY COLE (drums)
Chili Con Conga (vCC) / *Tarzan Of Harlem* (vCC) / *Jiveformation, Please* (vCC) / *Vuelva*

Wednesday 18 October 1939
Dizzy and the Cab Calloway Band close at the Audubon Theatre in New York City.

Thursday 19 October 1939
Dizzy and the Cab Calloway Band open a one-week engagement at the Carlton Theatre in Jamaica, New York.

Saturday 21 October 1939
Dizzy Gillespie's 22nd birthday.

Wednesday 25 October 1939
Dizzy and the Cab Calloway Band close at the Carlton Theatre in Jamaica, New York.

Tuesday 31 October 1939
Dizzy and the Cab Calloway Band open a one-week engagement at the Palace Theatre in Akron, Ohio.

Monday 6 November 1939
Dizzy and the Cab Calloway Band close at the Palace Theatre in Akron, Ohio.

Friday 10 November 1939
Dizzy and the Cab Calloway Band open a one-week engagement at the Fox Theatre in St. Louis, Missouri.

Thursday 16 November 1939
Dizzy and the Cab Calloway Band close at the Fox Theatre in St. Louis, Missouri.

Monday 20 November 1939
Dizzy records with the Cab Calloway Band in New York.
CAB CALLOWAY (vocal); DIZZY GILLESPIE, MARIO BAUZA, LAMAR WRIGHT (trumpets); CLAUDE JONES, KEG JOHNSON, DEPRIEST WHEELER (trombones); CHAUNCEY HAUGHTON, ANDREW BROWN (clarinet/alto sax); CHU BERRY, WALTER THOMAS (tenor sax); BENNY PAYNE (piano); DANNY BARKER (guitar); MILT HINTON (bass); COZY COLE (drums)
A Bee Gezindt (vCC) / *Give, Baby, Give* (vCC) / *Sincere Love* (vCC) / *Do It Again* (vCC)

Monday 27 November 1939
Dizzy and the Cab Calloway Band play a one-nighter in Joplin, Missouri.

Wednesday 29 November 1939
Dizzy and the Cab Calloway Band play a one-nighter in Wichita, Kansas.

Thursday 30 November 1939
Dizzy and the Cab Calloway Band play a one-nighter in the Municipal Auditorium in Kansas City, Missouri.

Friday 1 December 1939
Dizzy and the Cab Calloway Band open a one-week engagement at the Paramount Theatre in Omaha, Nebraska.

Thursday 7 December 1939
Dizzy and the Cab Calloway Band close at the Paramount Theatre in Omaha, Nebraska.

Friday 22 December 1939
Dizzy and the Cab Calloway Band open a one-week engagement at the Apollo Theatre in New York City.

Thursday 28 December 1939
Dizzy and the Cab Calloway Band close at the Apollo Theatre in New York City.

Friday 29 December 1939
Dizzy and the Cab Calloway Band open a one-week engagement at the Adams Theatre in Newark, New Jersey.

1940

Thursday 4 January 1940
Dizzy and the Cab Calloway Band close at the Adams Theatre in Newark, New Jersey.

Saturday 6 January 1940
Dizzy and the Cab Calloway Band play a dance at the Roseland State Ballroom in Boston.

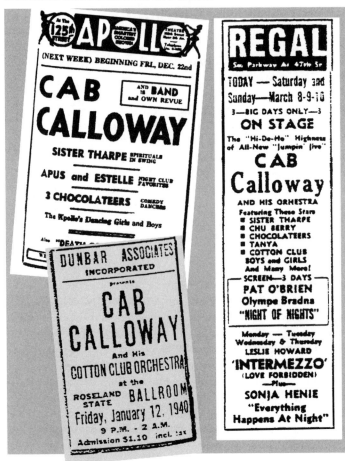

Friday 12 January 1940
Dizzy and the Cab Calloway Band play a dance at the Roseland State Ballroom in Boston.

Sunday 14 January 1940
Dizzy and the Cab Calloway Band play a one-nighter at the Chestnut Street Hall in Harrisburgh, Pennsylvania.

Saturday 17 February 1940
Dizzy and the Cab Calloway Band play a one-nighter at the Menorah Temple in Brooklyn, New York City.

Friday 8 March 1940
Dizzy records with the Cab Calloway Band in Chicago.
CAB CALLOWAY (vocal); DIZZY GILLESPIE, MARIO BAUZA, LAMAR WRIGHT (trumpets); TYREE GLENN (trombone/vibes); QUENTIN JACKSON, KEG JOHNSON (trombones); JERRY BLAKE (clarinet/alto sax); HILTON JEFFERSON, ANDREW BROWN (alto sax); CHU BERRY, WALTER THOMAS (tenor sax); BENNY PAYNE (piano); DANNY BARKER (guitar); MILT HINTON (bass); COZY COLE (drums)
Pickin' The Cabbage / Chop, Chop, Charlie Chan (vCC) / *Paradiddle / Boog It* (vCC)

The same day, Dizzy and the Cab Calloway Band open a three-day engagement at the Regal Theatre in Chicago.

Sunday 10 March 1940
Dizzy and the Cab Calloway Band close at the Regal Theatre in Chicago.

Friday 29 March 1940
Dizzy and the Cab Calloway Band open a one-week engagement at the Howard Theatre in Washington, D.C.

Thursday 4 April 1940
Dizzy and the Cab Calloway Band close at the Howard Theatre in Washington, D.C.

After Washington, Dizzy and the Cab Calloway Band open a long engagement at the Southland Café in Boston.

Thursday 9 May 1940
Dizzy and Lorraine Willis are married in Boston.

Wednesday 15 May 1940
Dizzy records with the Cab Calloway Band in New York City.
CAB CALLOWAY (vocal); DIZZY GILLESPIE, MARIO BAUZA, LAMAR WRIGHT (trumpets); TYREE GLENN (trombone/vibes); QUENTIN JACKSON, KEG JOHNSON (trombones); JERRY BLAKE (clarinet/alto sax); HILTON JEFFERSON, ANDREW BROWN (alto sax); CHU BERRY, WALTER THOMAS (tenor sax); BENNY PAYNE (piano); DANNY BARKER (guitar); MILT HINTON (bass); COZY COLE (drums)
Calling All Bars (2 takes) / *Do I Care? No, No* (vCC) / *The Lone Arranger / Feelin' Tip Top* (vCC) / *Topsy Turvy / Hi-De-Ho Serenade* (vCC) / *Who's Yehoodi?* (vCC, 2 takes)

Friday 17 May 1940
Dizzy and the Cab Calloway Band open a one-week engagement at the Apollo Theatre in New York City.

Thursday 23 May 1940
Dizzy and the Cab Calloway Band close at the Apollo Theatre in New York City.

Thursday 30 May 1940
Dizzy and the Cab Calloway Band play a dance at the Elks' Ballroom in Cambridge, Massachusetts.

Dizzy and the Cab Calloway Band play a tour of one-nighters through the south and midwest.

Shriners Blow Lids Carving Cozy Cole On Calloway Date
Memphis—Best bang of the month was Cab Calloway's two nites at the Rainbow Rollerdrome during the Shriners' convention. Impulsive Shriners blew their lids trying to carve Cozy Cole on drums (with firecrackers) to no avail.

DANCE **FAIRYLAND** SWIM
TONIGHT
Cab Calloway
AND HIS COTTON CLUB ORCHESTRA
DANCING FROM 9 P. M. TILL 6 P. M. BOX OFFICE 85c PLUS TAX
ADVANCE 70c PLUS TAX AT PARK TILL 6 P. M. BOX OFFICE 85c PLUS TAX
SWIM FOR HEALTH   In Crystal Filtered Water   25c
TUESDAY IS 2 FOR 1 DAY   Two people are admitted on any Ride or Dancing all evening with one paid adm.

Sunday 23 June 1940
Dizzy and the Cab Calloway Band play a one-nighter at Fairyland Park in Kansas City, Missouri.

Monday 24 June 1940
Dizzy is introduced to Charlie Parker who is working in the Kansas City area with Jay McShann's Band. They jam together at the local union building.

Thursday 27 June 1940
Dizzy records with the Cab Calloway Band in Chicago.
CAB CALLOWAY (vocal); DIZZY GILLESPIE, MARIO BAUZA, LAMAR WRIGHT (trumpets); TYREE GLENN (trombone/vibes); QUENTIN JACKSON, KEG JOHNSON (trombones); JERRY BLAKE (clarinet/alto sax); HILTON JEFFERSON, ANDREW BROWN (alto sax); CHU BERRY, WALTER THOMAS (tenor sax); BENNY PAYNE (piano); DANNY BARKER (guitar); MILT HINTON (bass); COZY COLE (drums)
Fifteen Minute Intermission (vCC) / *Rhapsody In Rhumba* (vCC) / *Come On With The 'Come On'* (vCC) / *A Ghost Of A Chance* (2 takes) / *Bye Bye Blues* (2 takes)
Dizzy also records with Alice O'Connell and the Glenn Hardman Trio for Columbia.
DIZZY GILLESPIE (trumpet); GLENN HARDMAN (organ); ISRAEL CROSBY (bass); COZY COLE (drums); ALICE O'CONNELL (vocal)
Once In A Lovetime (vAO) / *Shades Of Twilight* (vAO)

Friday 28 June 1940
Dizzy and the Cab Calloway Band open a one-week engagement at the State-Lake Theatre in Chicago.

Thursday 4 July 1940
Dizzy and the Cab Calloway Band close at the State-Lake Theatre in Chicago.

Friday 5 July 1940
Cab Calloway is in Detroit to audition young musicians for a junior Calloway Band.

Tuesday 16 July 1940
Dizzy and the Cab Calloway Band open at the Meadowbrook in Cedar Grove, New Jersey.

Saturday 27 July 1940
Dizzy and the Cab Calloway Band broadcast from the Meadowbrook in Cedar Grove, New Jersey.
CAB CALLOWAY (vocal); DIZZY GILLESPIE, MARIO BAUZA, LAMAR WRIGHT (trumpets); TYREE GLENN (trombone/vibes); QUENTIN JACKSON, KEG JOHNSON (trombones); JERRY BLAKE (clarinet/alto sax); HILTON JEFFERSON, ANDREW BROWN (alto sax); CHU BERRY, WALTER THOMAS (tenor sax); BENNY PAYNE (piano); DANNY BARKER (guitar); MILT HINTON (bass); COZY COLE (drums)
Minnie The Moocher (vCC) / *Limehouse Blues* / *I Can't Resist You* (vCC) / *Topsy Turvy* (vCC) / *Fifteen Minute Intermission* (vCC) / *I'll Pray For You* (vCC) / *Boog It* (vCC) / *Cupid's Nightmare* / *King Porter Stomp*

Monday 5 August 1940
Dizzy records with the Cab Calloway Band in New York.
CAB CALLOWAY (vocal); DIZZY GILLESPIE, MARIO BAUZA, LAMAR WRIGHT (trumpets); TYREE GLENN (trombone/vibes); QUENTIN JACKSON, KEG JOHNSON (trombones); JERRY BLAKE (clarinet/alto sax); HILTON JEFFERSON, ANDREW BROWN (alto sax); CHU BERRY, WALTER THOMAS (tenor sax); BENNY PAYNE (piano); DANNY BARKER (guitar); MILT HINTON (bass); COZY COLE (drums)
Papa's In Bed With His Britches On (vCC, 2 takes) / *Silly Old Moon* (vCC) / *Boo-Wah Boo-Wah* (vCC) / *Sunset* (vCC) / *Yo Eta Cansa*

Sunday 11 August 1940
Dizzy and the Cab Calloway Band close at the Meadowbrook in Cedar Grove, New Jersey.

Wednesday 14 August 1940
Dizzy and the Cab Calloway Band open a one-week engagement at the Paramount Theatre in New York City. Also on the bill are Avis Andrews, Stump & Stumpy, Cozy Cole and the Six Cotton Club Boys.

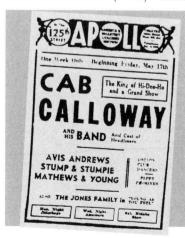

Tuesday 27 August 1940
Dizzy and the Cab Calloway Band close at the Paramount Theatre in New York City.

Wednesday 28 August 1940
Dizzy records with the Cab Calloway Band in New York. CAB CALLOWAY (vocal); DIZZY GILLESPIE, MARIO BAUZA, LAMAR WRIGHT (trumpets); TYREE GLENN (trombone/vibes); QUENTIN JACKSON, KEG JOHNSON (trombones); JERRY BLAKE (clarinet/alto sax); HILTON JEFFERSON, ANDREW BROWN (alto sax); CHU BERRY, WALTER THOMAS (tenor sax); BENNY PAYNE (piano); DANNY BARKER (guitar); MILT HINTON (bass); COZY COLE (drums)
Cupid's Nightmare / Levee Lullaby (vCC) / *Are You Hep To The Jive?* (vCC) / *Goin' Conga* (vCC) / *Hot Air / Lonesome Nights*

Sunday 15 September 1940
Down Beat reviews Cab Calloway's latest release:

Cab Calloway
"Ghost of a Chance" & "Come On With the Come On,"
Okeh 5687.
  Nice of Cab to give Chu Berry a whole side to demonstrate his ability on tenor. *Ghost* is all Chu, and wonderful Chu, but sounding in spots like he has been influenced considerably by Hawkins of late. There's also more Berry on the "B" side, plus a few bars of Dizzy Gillespie's trumpet, a full Calloway vocal, unfortunately, and nice clarinet bits. Note Cosy Cole's hide thumping—solid all the way but in good taste. Except for Cab, some nice jazz here.

Thursday 26 September 1940
Dizzy and the Cab Calloway Band open a one-week engagement at the Flatbush Theatre in Brooklyn, New York.

Wednesday 2 October 1940
Dizzy and the Cab Calloway Band close at the Flatbush Theatre in Brooklyn, New York.

Monday 14 October 1940
Dizzy records with the Cab Calloway Band in New York. CAB CALLOWAY (vocal); DIZZY GILLESPIE, MARIO BAUZA, LAMAR WRIGHT (trumpets); TYREE GLENN (trombone/vibes); QUENTIN JACKSON, KEG JOHNSON (trombones); JERRY BLAKE (clarinet/alto sax); HILTON JEFFERSON, ANDREW BROWN (alto sax); CHU BERRY, WALTER THOMAS (tenor sax); BENNY PAYNE (piano); DANNY BARKER (guitar); MILT HINTON (bass); COZY COLE (drums)

A Chicken Ain't Nothin' But A Bird (vCC, 2 takes) / *The Workers' Train* (vCC) / *North Of The Mohawk Trail* (vCC) / *Make Yourself At Home* (vCC)

Tuesday 15 October 1940
In a *Down Beat* review of Cab Calloway's recording of *Calling All Bars*, Dave Dexter says:

  Clever Benny Carter arrangement, disappointing Chu Berry tenor, good Dizzy Gillespie trumpet and a fairly strong beat. The band isn't as bad as most musicians make it out to be.

Thursday 17 October 1940
Dizzy registers for the draft at Lenox Avenue in Harlem.

Monday 21 October 1940
Dizzy Gillespie's 23rd birthday.

Friday 15 November 1940
Dizzy and the Cab Calloway Band open a one-week engagement at the Earle Theatre in Philadelphia.

Thursday 21 November 1940
Dizzy and the Cab Calloway Band close at the Earle Theatre in Philadelphia.

Friday 22 November 1940
Dizzy and the Cab Calloway Band open a one-week engagement at the Apollo Theatre in New York City.

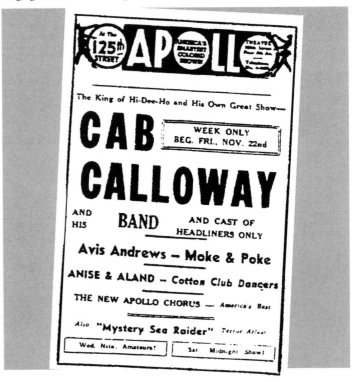

Thursday 28 November 1940
Dizzy and the Cab Calloway Band close at the Apollo Theatre in New York City.

1941

Thursday 16 January 1941
Dizzy records with the Cab Calloway Band in Chicago.
CAB CALLOWAY (vocal); DIZZY GILLESPIE, MARIO BAUZA, LAMAR WRIGHT (trumpets); TYREE GLENN (trombone/vibes); QUENTIN JACKSON, KEG JOHNSON (trombones); JERRY BLAKE (clarinet/alto sax); HILTON JEFFERSON, ANDREW BROWN (alto sax); CHU BERRY, WALTER THOMAS (tenor sax); BENNY PAYNE (piano); DANNY BARKER (guitar); MILT HINTON (bass); COZY COLE (drums)
Run Little Rabbit (vCC) / *Willow Weep For Me* / *You Are The One In My Heart* (vCC) / *All You All Reet?* (vCC) / *Ebony Silhouette*

Friday 24 January 1941
Dizzy and the Cab Calloway Band open a one-week engagement at the State-Lake Theatre in Chicago.

Thursday 30 January 1941
Dizzy and the Cab Calloway Band close at the State-Lake Theatre in Chicago.

Sunday 23 February 1941
Dizzy and the Cab Calloway Band open a one-week engagement at Topsy's Roost in Los Angeles.

Saturday 1 March 1941
Dizzy and the Cab Calloway Band close at Topsy's Roost in Los Angeles.

Wednesday 5 March 1941
Dizzy records with the Cab Calloway Band in New York.
CAB CALLOWAY (vocal); DIZZY GILLESPIE, JONAH JONES, LAMAR WRIGHT (trumpets); TYREE GLENN (trombone/vibes); QUENTIN JACKSON, KEG JOHNSON (trombones); JERRY BLAKE (clarinet/alto sax); HILTON JEFFERSON, ANDREW BROWN (alto sax); CHU BERRY, WALTER THOMAS (tenor sax); BENNY PAYNE (piano); DANNY BARKER (guitar); MILT HINTON (bass); COZY COLE (drums)
Hep Cat Love Song (vCC) / *Jonah Joins The Cab* (vCC, 2 takes) / *Geechee Joe* (vCC, 2 takes) / *Special Delivery* (2 takes)

During May Dizzy receives notification that he is classified 1-A (fit for active service) in the draft. He spends a lot of time after hours jamming at Monroe's Uptown House and Minton's Playhouse. Some of the sessions are recorded by enthusiast Jerry Newman:
DIZZY GILLESPIE, UNKNOWN (trumpets); DON BYAS (tenor sax); CHARLIE CHRISTIAN (guitar); NICK FENTON (bass); KENNY CLARKE OR HAROLD 'DOC' WEST (drums)
Up On Teddy's Hill
CHU BERRY (tenor sax) and a pianist replace Charlie Christian
Stardust
DIZZY GILLESPIE (trumpets), KENNY KERSEY (piano), NICK FENTON (bass), KENNY CLARKE (drums)
Stardust / *Kerouac*

Friday 16 May 1941
Dizzy and the Cab Calloway Band play the first of a two-night engagement at the New Washington Theatre in New York City. They share the bill with Louis Prima's Band.

Saturday 17 May 1941
Dizzy and the Cab Calloway Band conclude their two nights at the New Washington Theatre in New York City.

Friday 30 May 1941
Dizzy and the Cab Calloway Band open a four-week engagement in the Panther Room of the Hotel Sherman in Chicago (*below*).

Monday 16 June 1941
Dizzy and the Cab Calloway Band broadcast from the Panther Room in Chicago.
The Great Lie (Pantin' With The Panther) / Chu Berry Jam

Thursday 26 June 1941
Dizzy and the Cab Calloway Band close at the Panther Room of the Hotel Sherman in Chicago.

Sunday 29 June 1941
Dizzy and the Cab Calloway Band play a dance at the Savoy Ballroom in Chicago.

Thursday 3 July 1941
Dizzy records with the Cab Calloway Band in New York City.
Cab Calloway (vocal); Dizzy Gillespie, Jonah Jones, Lamar Wright (trumpets); Tyree Glenn (trombone/vibes); Quentin Jackson, Keg Johnson (trombones); Jerry Blake (clarinet/alto sax); Hilton Jefferson, Andrew Brown (alto sax); Chu Berry, Walter Thomas (tenor sax); Benny Payne (piano); Danny Barker (guitar); Milt Hinton (bass); Cozy Cole (drums)
Take The A Train / Chattanooga Choo-Choo (vCC) / *My Gal* (vCC) / *St. James Infirmary* (vCC)

Friday 4 July 1941
Dizzy and the Cab Calloway Band open a three-week engagement at the Strand Theatre in New York City. Also on the bill are Avis Andrews, Moke & Poke and Otto Eason.

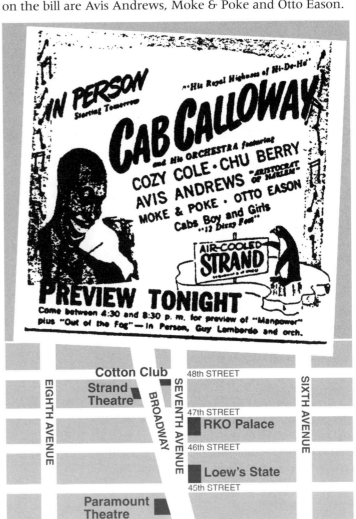

Monday 21 July 1941
Dizzy and the Cab Calloway Band play a Bathing Beauty Contest Ball at the Sonia Ballroom in Brooklyn, New York City. Also appearing are Canada Lee, Bill Robinson, Joe Bostic and Erskine Hawkins.

Thursday 24 July 1941
Dizzy records with the Cab Calloway Band in New York.
Cab Calloway (vocal); Dizzy Gillespie, Jonah Jones, Lamar Wright (trumpets); Tyree Glenn (trombone/vibes); Quentin Jackson, Keg Johnson (trombones); Jerry Blake (clarinet/alto sax); Hilton Jefferson, Andrew Brown (alto sax); Chu Berry, Walter Thomas (tenor sax); Benny Payne (piano); Danny Barker (guitar); Milt Hinton (bass); Cozy Cole (drums)
St. James Infirmary (vCC) / *We Go Well Together* (vCC) / *Hey Doc* (vCC, TG) / *I See A Million People* (vCC) / *Conchita* (vCC)

Dizzy and the Cab Calloway Band close at the Strand Theatre in New York City.

Friday 22 August 1941

Dizzy and the Cab Calloway Band open a one-week engagement at the Earle Theatre in Philadelphia.

Thursday 28 August 1941

Dizzy and the Cab Calloway Band close at the Earle Theatre in Philadelphia.

Monday 1 September 1941

Dave Dexter reviews the latest Cab Calloway release in *Down Beat*:

> Unaffected, forthright job on Bill Strayhorn's *Take the 'A' Train* is mostly ensemble, played well, with Chu's tenor and Diz Gillespie's horn bursting through for short solo bits. Neat stuff, neatly done. Cab sings the "B" side, *Chattanooga Choo Choo*, which we'll plant now and dig later. Okeh 6305.

Friday 5 September 1941

Dizzy and the Cab Calloway Band open a week-end engagement at the Palace Theatre in Canton, Ohio.

Sunday 7 September 1941

Dizzy and the Cab Calloway Band close at the Palace Theatre in Canton, Ohio.

Wednesday 10 September 1941

Dizzy records with the Cab Calloway Band in New York City.

CAB CALLOWAY (vocal); DIZZY GILLESPIE, JONAH JONES, LAMAR WRIGHT (trumpets); TYREE GLENN (trombone/vibes); QUENTIN JACKSON, KEG JOHNSON (trombones); JERRY BLAKE (clarinet/alto sax); HILTON JEFFERSON, ANDREW BROWN (alto sax); CHU BERRY, WALTER THOMAS (tenor sax); BENNY PAYNE (piano); DANNY BARKER (guitar); MILT HINTON (bass); COZY COLE (drums); PALMER BROTHERS (vocal)

Blues In The Night (vCC, PB, 2 takes) / *Mrs Finnigan* (vCC) / *My Coo-Coo Bird* (vCC) / *Says Who? Says You, Says I* (vCC)

Friday 19 September 1941

Dizzy and the Cab Calloway Band open a week-end engagement at the State Theatre in Hartford, Connecticut.

Sunday 21 September 1941

Dizzy and the Cab Calloway Band close at the State Theatre in Hartford, Connecticut. During the show, a spitball is thrown by one of the band during a Cab feature. Calloway blames Diz who pulls a knife on him. The result is that Dizzy Gillespie is fired from the band.

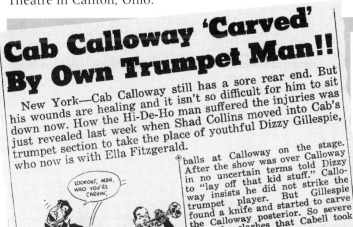

Cab Calloway 'Carved' By Own Trumpet Man!!

New York—Cab Calloway still has a sore rear end. But his wounds are healing and it isn't so difficult for him to sit down now. How the Hi-De-Ho man suffered the injuries was just revealed last week when Shad Collins moved into Cab's trumpet section to take the place of youthful Dizzy Gillespie, who now is with Ella Fitzgerald.

LOOKOUT, MAN, WHO YOU'RE CARVIN'.

Gillespie knifed Calloway, his boss, in a Hartford theater several weeks ago following an argument in which Calloway dressed him down for allegedly shooting spit-

balls at Calloway on the stage. After the show was over Calloway in no uncertain terms told Dizzy to "lay off that kid stuff." Calloway insists he did not strike the trumpet player. But Gillespie found a knife and started to carve the Calloway posterior. So severe were the slashes that Cabell took 10 stitches from a doctor.

Boys in the band, however, claim that Dizzy wasn't shooting spitballs on the stage. They say that little paper airplanes, sailed by the men in the band on the stage as part of an act, were thrown by Dizzy and that one of them struck Calloway while he was prancing about shouting "Yeah Mans" and "Skee-dee-dees" into a mike. Calloway was enraged, at any rate, and bawled out the young musician when the curtain dropped. The knifing followed.

Calloway and his band are still on tour. Their Sunday night Mutual system "Quizicale" program no longer is on the air. But Cab, with the best band of his career behind him, has been doing better business this year than any time since 1931 when his Hi-De-Ho magic first swept the nation. Gillespie, of course, was fired and joined Ella Fitzgerald, taking Taft Jordan's place. Collins' seat with the Calloway brass is only temporary, Calloway's managers pointed out.

And Cab's rear end is getting better.

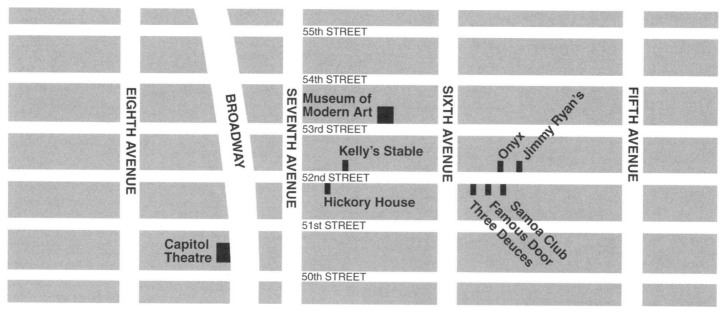

Sunday 5 October 1941
Dizzy joins Ella Fitzgerald and her Orchestra for a two-week engagement at Levaggi's Restaurant in Boston.

Saturday 18 October 1941
Dizzy and the Ella Fitzgerald Orchestra close at Levaggi's Restaurant in Boston.

Dizzy returns to New York and resumes his after-hours jamming at the Uptown House. Jerry Newman is there with his recording machine and captures Dizzy and a couple of other trumpeters on *The Dizzy Crawl*.

Tuesday 21 October 1941
Dizzy Gillespie's 24th birthday.

Wednesday 22 October 1941
Dizzy Gillespie joins the Benny Carter Band at the first of a series of 'Salon Swing' concerts at the Museum of Modern Art in New York City. Also on the bill are Maxine Sullivan and Teddy Wilson.

Dizzy Gillespie To Benny Carter

New York—Dizzy Gillespie, youthful trumpeter who recently parted company with Cab Calloway after an altercation backstage in a Hartford theater, now is blowing horn in Benny Carter's band.

Gillespie made his official bow with Carter at the first "Salon Swing" concert at the Museum of Modern Art which featured Carter's band and Maxine Sullivan.

Wednesday 29 October 1941
Dizzy Gillespie and the Benny Carter Band open at Kelly's Stable on 52nd Street in New York City. Also on the bill are Art Tatum and the King Cole Trio. The Carter band consists of: Benny Carter, alto sax; Dizzy Gillespie, trumpet; Al Gibson, clarinet; Sonny White, piano; John Collins, guitar; Charlie Drayton, bass, and Kenny Clarke, drums.

Sunday 7 December 1941
Japanese aircraft attack the U.S. Fleet at Pearl Harbour in Hawaii. 3000 Americans are killed and 19 ships are sunk or damaged.

Tuesday 9 December 1941
Dizzy Gillespie and the Benny Carter Band close at Kelly's Stable on 52nd Street in New York City.

Thursday 11 December 1941
Dizzy Gillespie and the Benny Carter Band open at the Famous Door on 52nd Street, backing Billie Holiday.

Monday 15 December 1941
Dizzy Gillespie joins the Charlie Barnet Orchestra for a two-week tour.

Dizzy Gillespie In Barnet Ork

New York—John (Dizzy) Gillespie was slated to join Charlie Barnet's ork as featured hot trumpeter about Dec. 15. He'll replace Bobby Burnet, who put himself on notice recently.

Gillespie's joining will not be permanent, however. Barnet plans to use the colored ace, who formerly was with Teddy Hill and Cab Calloway and who now is with Benny Carter, only for about three weeks on a tour.

Several of Barnet's men are on notice and the *status quo* of the entire band is reported to be very much of a question mark.

1942

January 1942
At the end of the Charlie Barnet tour, Dizzy Gillespie rejoins the Benny Carter Band at the Famous Door on 52nd Street in New York City.

Friday 9 January 1942
Charlie Parker and the Jay McShann band arrive in New York and open at the Savoy Ballroom in Harlem. Dizzy renews his friendship with Parker and they spend many hours together jamming after hours at Minton's Playhouse and Monroe's Uptown House.

Wednesday 4 February 1942
Benny Carter Band close at the Famous Door.

Benny Carter to Hit the Road

New York—Benny Carter will take a large ork out on the road about the last of February to do theaters in a unit which will also feature Maxine Sullivan and her songs. His band will have four trumpets, four saxes, four rhythm and no trombones.

Dizzy Gillespie has returned to the Carter fold on trumpet, Jimmy Hamilton is playing clarinet, replacing Al Gibson.

Miss Sullivan's South American tour was cancelled because of the war and the theater booking comes instead. Carter has been doing well with a small band at the Famous Door. He plays alto, tenor, trumpet and clary, and writes most of his crew's scores.

Sunday 8 February 1942
Dizzy appears at one of Harry Lim's Sunday afternoon jam sessions at the Village Vanguard in New York City.

Monday 9 February 1942
Dizzy records with Pete Brown and his Band for Decca in New York City.

DIZZY GILLESPIE (trumpet); JIMMY HAMILTON (clarinet); PETE BROWN (alto sax); SAMMY PRICE (piano); CHARLIE DRAYTON (bass); RAY NATHAN (drums); HELEN HUMES, NORA LEE KING (vocal)

Mound Bayou (vHH) / *Unlucky Woman* (vHH) / *Gonna Buy Me A Telephone* (vHH) / *Cannon Ball* (vNLK)

Friday 20 February 1942
Dizzy opens with the Fletcher Henderson Orchestra at the Apollo Theatre in New York City.

Thursday 26 February 1942
Dizzy and the Fletcher Henderson Orchestra close at the Apollo Theatre in New York City.

Dizzy also works with Claude Hopkins and Fess Williams around this time, and sells arrangements to Jimmy Dorsey (*Grand Central Getaway*) and Woody Herman (*Down Under, Swing Shift* and *Woody'n' You*).

Below: Dizzy compares pipes at one of Harry Lim's Sunday afternoon jam sessions at the Village Vanguard. L to r: Dizzy, Harry Lim, Vido Musso, Billy Kyle, Cootie Williams, Charlie Shavers, and Johnny Williams.

Dizzy Gillespie Joins Les Hite

When Les Hite went into a period of intensive rehearsal after concluding his booking at the Brooklyn Strand Theatre last week, he had a new man in each section of the band—trumpet, trombone, reed and rhythm.

One of the new men was Gerald Wiggins, a young piano discovery whom Les heard accompanying Stepin Fetchit at the theatre before the comedian's abrupt departure from the show. Wiggins replaces Coney Woodman, who was drafted. His brother, Britt Woodman, also gone with the draft, was succeeded by a trombonist from Baltimore named Leon Comegys.

In the saxophone team, Johnny Brown took Sol Moore's place on baritone sax. Most important of the changes was the acquisition of John "Dizzy" Gillespie, quixotic young man with a horn recently heard with Benny Carter and Charlie Barnet. He replaced Stumpy Whitlock, who went back to his home in Omaha.

GALA RE-OPENING FRIDAY, SEPT. 4TH

HARLEM'S HIGH SPOT

APOLLO

WEEK ONLY—BEG. FRI. SEPT. 4TH

AMERICA'S GREATEST QUARTETTE

4 INK SPOTS

LUCKY AND HIS BAND **MILLINDER**

SISTER THARPE

TREVOR BACON · EDWARD SISTERS
JESSE AND JAMES · TIM MOORE

WED. NIGHT AMATEUR BROADCAST | SAT. MIDNIGHT SHOW

Monday 1 April 1942

Dizzy joins Les Hite Orchestra immediately after Britt and Coney Woodman are drafted as the band closes at the Strand Theatre in Brooklyn. Dizzy replaces Stumpy Whitlock. The band go on a tour of New England.

May 1942

Dizzy records with Les Hite's Orchestra in New York City.
LES HITE (director/alto sax/vocal); DIZZY GILLESPIE, JOE WILDER, WALTER WILLIAMS (trumpets); LEON COMEGYS, ALLEN DUNHAM, ALFRED COBBS (trombones); JOHN BROWN, FLOYD TURNHAM (alto sax); QUEDELLIS MARTYN, ROGER HURD (tenor sax); SOL MOORE (baritone sax); GERRY WIGGINS (piano); FRANK PASLEY (guitar); BENNY BOOKER (bass); OSCAR BRADLEY (drums); JIMMY ANDERSON (vocal)
I Remember You (vJA) / *Jersey Bounce* / *Idaho* (vLH) / *One Dozen Roses* (vJA)

Tuesday 19 May 1942

Dizzy leaves the Les Hite Orchestra when it returns to the West Coast.

Wednesday 20 May 1942

Dizzy sits in with the Woody Herman Orchestra for a one-week engagement at the Paramount Theatre in New York.

Saturday 30 May 1942

Dizzy and Tab Smith join Lucky Millinder's Band at the Savoy Ballroom in Harlem. They are resident at the ballroom into August but manage to fit in other gigs.

Friday 12 June 1942

Dizzy and the Lucky Millinder Band open a one-week engagement at the Apollo Theatre in New York City.

Thursday 18 June 1942

Dizzy and the Lucky Millinder Band close at the Apollo Theatre in New York City.

Thursday 25 June 1942

Dizzy and the Lucky Millinder Band play a benefit at the Golden Gate Ballroom in New York City.

Saturday 25 July 1942

Dizzy and the Lucky Millinder Band play a benefit at the Majestic Theatre in Brooklyn.

Wednesday 29 July 1942

Dizzy records with Lucky Millinder's Band in New York.

DIZZY GILLESPIE, WILLIAM SCOTT, NELSON BRYANT (trumpets); GEORGE STEVENSON, JOE BRITTON (trombones); TAB SMITH, BILLY BOWEN (alto sax); STAFFORD SIMON, DAVE YOUNG (tenor sax); ERNEST PURCE (baritone sax); BILL DOGGETT (piano); TREVOR BACON (guitar/vocal); NICK FENTON (bass); PANAMA FRANCIS (drums)
Are You Ready? (vTB) / *Mason Flyer* / *When The Lights Go On Again* (vTB) / *Little John Special*

Friday 4 September 1942

Dizzy and the Lucky Millinder Band open a one-week engagement at the Apollo Theatre in New York City. The Ink Spots are also on the bill.

Thursday 10 September 1942

Dizzy and the Lucky Millinder Band close at the Apollo Theatre in New York City.

Friday 11 September 1942

Dizzy and the Lucky Millinder Band open a one-week engagement at the Adams Theatre in Newark, New Jersey.

Thursday 17 September 1942

Dizzy and the Lucky Millinder Band close at the Adams Theatre in Newark, New Jersey.

Friday 18 September 1942

Dizzy and the Lucky Millinder Band open a one-week engagement at the Fox Theatre in Brooklyn, New York.

Thursday 24 September 1942

Dizzy and the Lucky Millinder Band close at the Fox Theatre in Brooklyn, New York.

Friday 25 September 1942

Dizzy and the Lucky Millinder Band open a one-week engagement at the Earle Theatre in Philadelphia. During this engagement, Lucky gives Dizzy two weeks notice, telling him that he'd "lost his chops." Dizzy plays his heart out for the rest of the week and Lucky asks him to stay on, but Dizzy has already got himself a job at Nat Segal's Downbeat Club in Philadelphia.

Thursday 1 October 1942

Dizzy and the Lucky Millinder Band close at the Earle Theatre in Philadelphia.

After leaving Lucky Millinder, Dizzy has a seven-week contract at the Downbeat Club in Philadelphia. He earns $150 a week playing with a local trio. 16-yr-old drummer Stan Levey sits in and eventually joins the group.

DIZZY FORMS BAND

in Philadelphia. Gillespie, former Calloway and Millinder trumpeter, is leading a small all-colored combination at the Downbeat Club.

Philadelphia—Still on tap at the Downbeat club is Dizzy Gillespie's group. The former Calloway trumpeter is proving popular by remaining for the umpteenth week. With him are Johnny Acea on piano, William Smith, on bass and Frankie Snyder, drums. Snyder, the only white member, also does vocals.

Wednesday 21 October 1942

Dizzy Gillespie's 25th birthday.

Dizzy stays with his mother in Philadelphia, but travels into New York each Sunday to see Lorraine and join in the jam sessions at Jimmy Ryan's and Kelly's Stable.

1943

Saturday 9 January 1943

Dizzy appears at a Swing Concert at the Savoy Ballroom in New York City.

When the Earl Hines Orchestra comes through Philly at the end of January, Billy Eckstine gets Dizzy into the band. Charlie Parker joins on tenor sax shortly afterwards.

Tuesday 2 February 1943

Dizzy and the Earl Hines Orchestra play a one-nighter at the Robbins Theatre in Warren, Ohio.

Friday 5 February 1943

Dizzy and the Earl Hines Orchestra open a one-week engagement at the Paradise Theatre in Detroit.

Thursday 11 February 1943

Dizzy and the Earl Hines Orchestra close at the Paradise Theatre in Detroit.

Saturday 13 February 1943

Dizzy and the Earl Hines Orchestra play a one-nighter at the Auditorium in Dayton, Ohio.

Sunday 14 February 1943

Dizzy and the Earl Hines Orchestra play a Valentine Night dance at the Savoy Ballroom in Chicago. There are three shooting incidents during the dance.

EARL 'FATHER' HINES
(Reviewed at the Savoy Ballroom, Chicago)

Although most of the huge crowd which packed the Savoy for Father's South Side appearance was confused throughout the evening as to whether they were in a ballroom or a shooting gallery (there were three shootings within an hour), the Hines band played to one of South Side's largest and most enthusiastic crowds in months Valentine's Day.

Hines, far from having a subtle band to begin with, played over the roof at the Savoy. The band was completely wild and, though precision may have been lacking in much of the band's work, solos echoed the crowd's exuberance and the whole evening entered early into a state of primitive enthusiasm which left neither the band nor the crowd throughout the evening.

Earl, though truly ill from a bad siege of one-nighters in an equally bad siege of weather, sparked the band with his, as always, magnificent piano, as Shorty McConnell went out of the world playing lusty, vigorous, and imaginative trumpet to lead the remainder of the soloists through the evening.

Altoist Angie Gardner and bassist Jesse Simpkins were, to our way of thinking, two of the best boys in the band. Angie is given little chance to solo, but plays precision horn with cleaner pattern structure than anyone in the band but Earl. Lacking some of the fervor, possibly, of the approved Hines soloists, he more than makes up for it in his ability and in ideas. Jesse plays bass very like the late Jimmy Blanton behind Earl's piano. The boy is fine. Benny Green shone in the trombone section.

Billy Eckstein of course stole the show with his excellent blues. Billy has that intangible ability to combine, not shouting, but tone in blues and still keep the blue feeling predominant. Blues shouters have a sincerity and warmth usually lost in the voice of a good singer, and yet lack tone sweetness. Billy combines both incomparably.

Madeline Green, excellent as ever, is now sharing vocals with Sarah Vaughn, a newcomer to the band with a pleasing voice and a subtle style.

It's hard to describe the band without using the word 'wild.' I've always had that trouble in writing about the Hines band. It has an unquenchable madness in its soul that seems to exert itself from theme to theme. Earl likes it. The fellows like it. The crowd likes it and…well, so do I, darn it.

Monday 15 February 1943

Dizzy and Charlie Parker are recorded by Bob Redcross in Room 305 of the Savoy Hotel in Chicago.

DIZZY GILLESPIE (trumpet); CHARLIE PARKER (alto sax); OSCAR PETTIFORD (bass); SHADOW WILSON (drums)
Sweet Georgia Brown 1 / Sweet Georgia Brown 2

Tuesday 23 February 1943
Dizzy and the Earl Hines Orchestra open a 4-night engagement at the Tune Town Ballroom in St. Louis.

Friday 26 February 1943
Dizzy and the Earl Hines Orchestra close at the Tune Town Ballroom in St. Louis.

Saturday 27 February 1943
Dizzy and the Earl Hines Orchestra play a one-nighter at the Ashland Avenue Auditorium in Chicago.

Thursday 4 March 1943
Dizzy and the Earl Hines Orchestra open a one-week engagement at the Adams Theatre in Newark, New Jersey.

Wednesday 10 March 1943
Dizzy and the Earl Hines Orchestra close at the Adams Theatre in Newark, New Jersey.

Friday 12 March 1943
Dizzy and the Earl Hines Orchestra open a one-week engagement at Fays Theatre in Philadelphia.

Thursday 18 March 1943
Dizzy and the Earl Hines Orchestra close at Fays Theatre in Philadelphia.

Friday 19 March 1943
Dizzy and the Earl Hines Orchestra play a dance at the South State Armory in Boston.

Sunday 21 March 1943
Dizzy and the Earl Hines Orchestra play a Victory Ball at the Portland Elk's Club in Portland, Maine.

Friday 2 April 1943
Dizzy and the Earl Hines Orchestra open a one-week engagement at the Howard Theatre in Washington, D.C.

Thursday 8 April 1943
Dizzy and the Earl Hines Orchestra close at the Howard Theatre in Washington, D.C.

Sunday 11 April 1943
Dizzy and the Earl Hines Orchestra play a one-nighter at the Lincoln Colonnades in Washington, D.C.

Sunday 18 April 1943
Dizzy and the Earl Hines Orchestra play a one-nighter at the Memorial Auditorium in Buffalo.

Friday 23 April 1943
Dizzy and the Earl Hines Orchestra open a one-week engagement at the Apollo Theatre in New York City. Also on the bill are Bill Bailey, Tim Moore and Spick & Span.

Sunday 25 April 1943
Dizzy and the Earl Hines Orchestra play an afternoon dance at the Manhattan Center in New York City.

Thursday 29 April 1943
Dizzy and the Earl Hines Orchestra close at the Apollo Theatre in New York.

Below: The Earl Hines Band at the Apollo. Dizzy Gillespie (far left), Charlie Parker (far right).

Saturday 8 May 1943
Dizzy and the Earl Hines Orchestra play a Blue Ribbon Salute in a Galaxy of Stars at the Golden Gate Ballroom in New York City. Ralph Cooper emcees the show which features Louis Jordan & his Band, Bill Bailey, Lillian Fitzgerald and Patterson & Jackson. The Earl Hines Orchestra and Louis Jordan's Band embark on a Blue Ribbon tour of Army camps through the south and midwest. One night, a redneck hits Dizzy on the head with a bottle. Charlie Parker admonishes the assailant, *'You took advantage of my friend, you cur!'*

Saturday 19 June 1943
Dizzy and the Earl Hines Orchestra open a three-day engagement at the Municipal Auditorium in Kansas City, Missouri.

Monday 21 June 1943
Dizzy and the Earl Hines Orchestra close at the Municipal Auditorium in Kansas City, Missouri.

Friday 9 July 1943
Dizzy and the Earl Hines Orchestra open a one-week engagement at the Apollo Theatre in New York City.

Thursday 15 July 1943
Dizzy and the Earl Hines Orchestra close at the Apollo Theatre in New York City.

Friday 16 July 1943
Dizzy and the Earl Hines Orchestra play a concert at the Town Hall in Philadelphia.

Saturday 17 July 1943
Dizzy and the Earl Hines Orchestra play a dance at the Manhattan Center in New York City.

Sunday 18 July 1943
Dizzy and the Earl Hines Orchestra open a one-week engagement at the Tic Toc Club in Boston.

Saturday 24 July 1943
Dizzy and the Earl Hines Orchestra close at the Tic Toc Club in Boston.

Sunday 25 July 1943
Dizzy and the Earl Hines Orchestra play a concert at the Palace Theatre, Brooklyn followed by a dance at the Renaissance Ballroom in Harlem.

Friday 30 July 1943
Dizzy and the Earl Hines Orchestra open a one-week engagement at the Howard Theatre in Washington, D.C.

Thursday 5 August 1943
Dizzy and the Earl Hines Orchestra close at the Howard Theatre in Washington, D.C.

Above: The Dizzy Gillespie Quintet at the Onyx Club on 52nd Street. L to r: Hal West (drums), Lester Young (tenor sax), Oscar Pettiford (bass), George Wallington (piano), Dizzy (trumpet). Dizzy is doubling with the Duke Ellington at the Capitol Theatre.

Friday 6 August 1943
Dizzy and the Earl Hines Orchestra open a one-week engagement at the Royal Theatre in Baltimore.

Thursday 12 August 1943
Dizzy and the Earl Hines Orchestra close at the Royal Theatre in Baltimore. Dizzy, Parker and Eckstine quit.

Saturday 11 September 1943
Dizzy appears before a draft selection board in New York, is rejected and re-classified 4-F.

Thursday 14 October 1943
Dizzy Gillespie joins the Duke Ellington Orchestra for the 4-week engagement at the Capitol Theatre in New York City. He temporarily replaces Harold Baker who is not a member of Local 802. Also on the bill are Lena Horne, Peg Leg Bates, Patterson & Jackson and the Deep River Boys.

Wednesday 20 October 1943
Dizzy Gillespie Quintet open at the Onyx Club on 52nd Street. Lester Young is on tenor sax, with Oscar Pettiford (bass), Max Roach (drums) and George Wallington (piano). Billie Holiday and the Pete Brown Band are already resident at the Onyx. Dizzy is doubling with the Duke Ellington Orchestra at the Capitol Theatre.

Thursday 21 October 1943
Dizzy Gillespie's 26th birthday.

Monday 8 November 1943
After the show at the Capitol Theatre, on Dizzy's off-night at the Onyx, Duke Ellington's Orchestra record for World Broadcasting Transcriptions in a session that lasts all night.
DUKE ELLINGTON (piano); TAFT JORDAN, WALLACE JONES, DIZZY GILLESPIE (trumpet); REX STEWART (cornet); JOE NANTON, LAWRENCE BROWN, CLAUDE JONES (trombone); JIMMY HAMILTON (clarinet/tenor sax); JOHNNY HODGES (clarinet/soprano sax/alto sax); OTTO HARDWICK (alto sax/bass sax); SKIPPY WILLIAMS (tenor sax); HARRY CARNEY (clarinet/alto sax/baritone sax); FRED GUY (guitar); JUNIOR RAGLIN (bass); SONNY GREER (drums); AL HIBBLER (vocal)
Rockin' In Rhythm (5 takes) / *Blue Skies* (6 takes) / *Boy Meets Horn* (2 takes) / *Do Nothin' Till You Hear From Me* (vAH, 3 takes) / *Summertime* (vAH, 2 takes) / *Sentimental Lady* (2 takes) / *Tea For Two* (2 takes) / *C-Jam Blues* / *Hop Skip Jump* / *Mood Indigo* (2 takes)

Wednesday 10 November 1943
The Duke Ellington Orchestra close at the Capitol Theatre in New York City ending Dizzy's tenure with the band. Dizzy continues to lead his group at the Onyx.

Wednesday 1 December 1943
Lester Young rejoins Count Basie at the Lincoln Hotel in New York City. His replacement is Don Byas as the Dizzy Gillespie Quintet continue their long engagement at the Onyx Club on 52nd Street. Billie Holiday also leaves the Onyx around this time.

52nd Street's Newest Swing Sensation
THE ONYX CLUB in 52nd Street is scoring nightly with the new John (Dizzy) Gillespie Band, led by Gillespie, former trumpet ace with Cab Calloway. Others in the outfit are Max Roach, drums; Don Byas, tenor; Oscar Pettiford, bass; and Billy Taylor, piano.

1944

Gillespie Heads Groovy Combo
New York—Dizzy Gillespie's trumpet is setting the pace at the Onyx Club here with a five piece unit, which is booked by the William Morris agency. Group contains Don Byas, who left Count Basie when tenorman Lester Young returned; and Oscar Pettiford, Charlie Barnet's bass find.

Wednesday 16 February 1944
Dizzy records with Coleman Hawkins and his Orchestra for Apollo in New York City.
DIZZY GILLESPIE, VIC COULSON, ED VANDEVER (trumpets); LEO PARKER, LEONARD LOWRY (alto sax); COLEMAN HAWKINS, DON BYAS, RAY ABRAMS (tenor sax); BUDD JOHNSON (baritone sax); CLYDE HART (piano); OSCAR PETTIFORD (bass); MAX ROACH (drums)
Woody'n You / *Bu-Dee-Daht* / *Yesterdays*

Tuesday 22 February 1944
Dizzy records with Coleman Hawkins and his Orchestra for Apollo in New York City.
DIZZY GILLESPIE, VIC COULSON, ED VANDEVER (trumpets); LEO PARKER, LEONARD LOWRY (alto sax); COLEMAN HAWKINS, DON BYAS, RAY ABRAMS (tenor sax); BUDD JOHNSON (baritone sax); CLYDE HART (piano); OSCAR PETTIFORD (bass); MAX ROACH (drums)
Disorder At The Border / *Feeling Zero* / *Rainbow Mist (Body And Soul)*

Budd Johnson replaces Don Byas and later Clyde Hart replaces George Wallington in the Quintet which continues its run at the Onyx.

A coastguard stationed in Brooklyn writes to *Down Beat*:

Gillespie Great
To the Editor,

In reading the interesting article on Hawkins in the *Beat*, I was reminded of another musician who is adding a new and refreshing style to jazz. Anyone who heard Dizzy Gillespie recently at the Onyx club realizes that Dizzy is contributing something new to jazz. In visits there, I noticed that Coleman Hawkins was often present to hear Dizzy blow. Such recognition means Dizzy must be good.

Dizzy and musicians like him deserve recognition. In musicians of such caliber lies the future of good jazz. At present, I think we ought to promote such men, because jazz is at a standstill.

March 1944
Early in March there is a split between Dizzy and Oscar Pettiford. Pettiford remains at the Onyx with Joe Guy (trumpet), Johnny Hartzfield (tenor sax), Joe Springer (piano), and Harold West (drums). Dizzy crosses the street to the Yacht Club (formerly the Famous Door) with Budd Johnson (tenor sax), Clyde Hart (piano), Leonard Gaskin (bass) and Max Roach (drums). The band alternates with Trummy Young's Jump Band and Billy X-tine. Max Roach soon leaves and is replaced by Jackie Mills.

Pettiford Leads Onyx Club Band

New York—Shakeup at the Onyx Club finds Oscar Pettiford leading the featured combo, with Diz Gillespie, Bud Johnson, and Clyde Hart cutting across the street to the Yacht Club to alternate with Trummie Young's sextet.

Pettiford, who was featured with Diz' crew, has brought in Harold West, Eldridge's ex-tubman, Joe Springer on piano, and Franz Jackson, tenor, to continue the Onyx' presentation of top talent, including Billie Holiday, the Al Casey trio, and Toy Wilson, pianist.

Gillespie has Leonard Gaskin on bass and Jackie Mills on drums.

Thursday 13 April 1944

Dizzy records with Billy Eckstine and the Deluxe All Stars for Deluxe Records in New York City.

DIZZY GILLESPIE, AL KILLIAN, SHORTY MCCONNELL, FREDDIE WEBSTER (trumpets); CLAUDE JONES, HOWARD SCOTT, TRUMMY YOUNG (trombones); BUDD JOHNSON, JIMMY POWELL (alto sax); WARDELL GRAY, THOMAS CRUMP (tenor sax); RUDY RUTHERFORD (baritone sax); CLYDE HART (piano); CONNIE WAINWRIGHT (guitar); OSCAR PETTIFORD (bass); SHADOW WILSON (drums); BILLY ECKSTINE (vocal)

I Got A Date With Rhythm / I Stay In The Mood For You / Good Jelly Blues

Wednesday 26 April 1944

Coleman Hawkins and his band open at the Yacht Club in New York City to share the bill with Dizzy Gillespie and Budd Johnson. Billy Eckstine, billed as X-tine, is also on the bill.

April 1944

A 30% entertainment tax is introduced on spots classified as cabarets and the Yacht Club folds. By May it is sold and reopens as the Downbeat.

Below: A jam session at the newly opened Downbeat features (l to r): Freddy Webster, Sid Catlett, Scoops Carry, Trummy Young, Leonard Gaskin, Budd Johnson, Snags Allen, Dizzy and Harold 'Doc' West.

May 1944

Dizzy joins the John Kirby Band at the Aquarium, but is soon replaced by Emmett Berry.

Friday 19 May 1944

Dizzy and the John Kirby Orchestra broadcast from the Aquarium in New York City.

DIZZY GILLESPIE (trumpet); BUSTER BAILEY (clarinet); GEORGE JOHNSON (alto sax); BEN WEBSTER (tenor sax); RAM RAMIREZ (piano); JOHN KIRBY (bass); BILL BEASON (drums)

Close Shave / Takin' A Chance On Love / Yesterdays / Honeysuckle Rose

Monday 22 May 1944

Dizzy and the John Kirby Orchestra broadcast from the Aquarium in New York City.

DIZZY GILLESPIE (trumpet); BUSTER BAILEY (clarinet); GEORGE JOHNSON (alto sax); BEN WEBSTER (tenor sax); RAM RAMIREZ (piano); JOHN KIRBY (bass); BILL BEASON (drums)

I'm Coming Home / Yesterdays / Oh What A Beautiful Morning / Rose Room

Dizzy attends Coleman Hawkins' second celebrity party jam session at the Downbeat Club on 52nd Street in New York.

Wednesday 24 May 1944

Dizzy and the John Kirby Orchestra broadcast from the Aquarium in New York City.

DIZZY GILLESPIE (trumpet); BUSTER BAILEY (clarinet); GEORGE JOHNSON (alto sax); BEN WEBSTER (tenor sax); RAM RAMIREZ (piano); JOHN KIRBY (bass); BILL BEASON (drums)

Irresistible You / Perdido / Rose Room

Dizzy leaves John Kirby and joins Billy Eckstine's Band as musical director. Dizzy also leads the trumpet section with Charlie Parker playing first alto.

Friday 9 June 1944

The Billy Eckstine Band's first date is a theatre date in Wilmington, Delaware. Dizzy falls asleep on the train and ends up in Washington, D.C., missing the first show. Drummer Shadow Wilson also fails to show.

> *NOW I'M REALLY FRANTIC. I DON'T HAVE DIZ THERE AND I DON'T HAVE ANY DRUMS. WE WORKED FOR A WEEK WITHOUT A DRUMMER. WHEN WE GOT TO TAMPA, FLORIDA, I PICKED UP A KID CALLED JOE, WHO PLAYED DRUMS.*

Saturday 24 June 1944

Dizzy appears at Music Dial's 1st Anniversary Breakfast Dance and Jam Session at the Golden Gate Ballroom in New York City. Ralph Cooper emcees the midnight show which also features Al Cooper's Savoy Sultans, Billie Holiday and the Art Tatum Trio.

July/August 1944

Dizzy and Billy Eckstine's Band play a two-week engagement at the Riviera Club in St. Louis. Trumpeter Buddy Anderson has contracted tuberculosis and is forced to leave the band. 18-year-old Miles Davis substitutes, but is not retained when the band move on to Chicago.

Friday 18 August 1944

Dizzy and Billy Eckstine's Band open a one-week engagement at the Regal Theatre in Chicago.

Eckstine Spots Strong Trumpets

Chicago—Billy Eckstine's trumpet quartet grabbed the spotlight during the band's stay at the Regal theater here. Thesection was composed of: Dizzy Gillespie, Howard McGhee, Gail Brockman and Marion Hazel. McGhee, subbing in Eckstine's band, has recently been featured soloist with Georgie Auld's ofay crew.

Remaining personnel includes: Charley Parker and John Jackson, altos; Eugene Ammons, son of Al Ammons, and Lucky Thompson, tenors; Leo Parker, baritone; Gerald Valentine, Arnett Sparrow and Rudy Morrison, trombones; John Malachi, piano; Tommy Potter, bass; and Art Blakey, drums, and Sara Vaughn, vocals.

The band plays some terrific double-timed specials, such as *Salt Peanuts, Night in Tunisia* and *Blitz*, all arranged by Dizzy Gillespie. Gerald Valentine is scoring the ballads. The Eckstine crew is slated for another recording session for DeLuxe label on Sept. 15, at which time they will cut six sides.

BILLY ECKSTINE
(Reviewed at the Regal Theater, Chicago)

Raymond Scott would enjoy this new band, for it's playing the type of visionary swing that the CBS maestro has been trying to concoct for the past five years. The ex-Hines blues singer has achieved the dream of a leader in only two months—a well-balanced group of top sidemen playing brilliant, revolutionary arrangements well.

The handsome "sepia Sinatra" is proving a versatile frontman. Besides his subtle performance with the blues while his contemporaries are shouting them, Billy is blowing some adequate trumpet with his section and is ingratiating himself to his fans with his relaxed stage presence.

Not far behind the leader is ever-muggin' Dizzy Gillespie. Record collectors have long watched for the ex-Calloway trumpeter's advanced ideas of improvisation. In writing the book for the crew's jumpers, Gillespie has inserted many of these fast riffs into the four-way trumpet parts. With men like Gail Brockman, Marion Hazel and Shorts McConnell blowing the trumpets are worth a long listen.

Driving force behind the reeds is Charley Parker, destined to take his place beside Hodges as a stylist on alto sax. After hearing this band do six shows during the week at the Regal, your reviewer didn't hear repeats on many of the choruses which Parker did. His tone is adequate, but the individualizing factor is his tremendous store of new ideas. Lucky Thompson, who plays one of the fastest horns in the business, and Eugene Ammons share tenor breaks.

Double-tempoed jumpers like those which stylize the Eckstine aggregation require a fast tubman like Art Blakey. Blakey's one-hand roll keeps the rhythm driving during even the fastest number. Pianist John Malachi and bassist Tommy Potter, who have played together since Washington, D. C., high school days, keep the section coordinated.

With Sara Vaughn doing pops like Gerald Valentine's *I'll Wait and Pray*, the sweet department is well taken care of. Eckstine draws plenty of swoons with his vocalizing on the standards.

Thursday 24 August 1944
Dizzy and Billy Eckstine's Band close at the Regal Theatre in Chicago.

Wednesday 30 August 1944
Dizzy and Billy Eckstine's Band play a dance (9.00pm–2.00am) at the Asbury Park Armory in Asbury Park, New Jersey.

Sunday 3 September 1944
Dizzy and Billy Eckstine's Band open a one-week engagement at the Tic Toc Club in Boston.

Above: Dizzy steps out front to solo with the Billy Eckstine Band at the Tic Toc Club in Boston. Also visible are drummer Art Blakey and, sitting behind Eckstine, tenor saxophonist Lucky Thompson.

Saturday 9 September 1944
Dizzy and Billy Eckstine's Band close at the Tic Toc Club in Boston.

Friday 15 September 1944
Dizzy and Billy Eckstine's Band open a one-week engagement at the Howard Theatre in Washington, D.C.

Thursday 21 September 1944
Dizzy and Billy Eckstine's Band close at the Howard Theatre in Washington, D.C. Dexter Gordon joins the band on the last night at the Howard Theatre.

Friday 22 September 1944
Dizzy and Billy Eckstine's Band open a one-week engagement at the Apollo Theatre in New York City. Also on the bill are Leroy, Leroy & Juanita and Doris Smart.

Leonard Feather reviews the show for *Metronome*:

BILLY ECKSTINE
Dizzy Heights
Apollo Theatre, New York

Billy Eckstine made an impression from the first moment when the curtains parted to reveal him, clothed in a brilliant white smile and suit, conducting a band of four trumpets, three trombones, five reeds and four rhythm.

Billy's personality and singing sold the show commercially; Dizzy Gillespie's musicianship and fine arrangements did most for it musically, though there were plenty of others to whom credit is due. For a young band, this bunch kicks wonderfully. In this short space all I can do is list the credits briefly:—

Shorty McConnell, with leader Billy towering over him as he blew some quiet but incisive trumpet on *Second Balcony Jump*. Gene Ammons, son of Albert the b-w man, blowing several choruses of terrific tenor and getting a heartwarming hand for it. Chippy Aulcott's trombone on the attractive Dizzy original *Night in Tunisia*. Johnny Jackson's alto work. Dizzy himself, announced by Eckstine as "the magic voice of the 52nd Street sewers," stepping down front to take a "vocal" on *Salt Peanuts* which consisted simply of repeating the title 12 times.

Dizzy's musicomic effects with the other three trumpets adding wit to good music in *Jelly Jelly*, and Eckstine adding his own horn to make it a five-trumpet climax. The fine drumming of Art Blakey; John Malachi's intelligent piano; the Lester Youthful tenor of Dexter Gordon.

Eckstine, needless to add, got a hand as he began to sing each juke-box hit, and could have stayed onstage all night. More surprising and very gratifying was the reception accorded to Sara Vaughn, Billy's superb *chanteuse*. What style, what phrasing, what control! Ah, *mon vieux*, this chick is groovy!

Thursday 28 September 1944

Dizzy and Billy Eckstine's Band close at the Apollo Theatre in New York City.

Friday 29 September 1944

Dizzy and Billy Eckstine's Band open a one-week engagement at the Royal Theatre in Baltimore.

Thursday 5 October 1944

Dizzy and Billy Eckstine's Band close at the Royal Theatre in Baltimore.

Friday 20 October 1944

Dizzy and Billy Eckstine's Band open a two-week engagement at Club Bali in Washington, D.C.

Saturday 21 October 1944

Dizzy Gillespie's 27th birthday.

Thursday 2 November 1944

Dizzy and Billy Eckstine's Band close at Club Bali in Washington, D.C.

Friday 3 November 1944

Dizzy and Billy Eckstine's Band open a one-week engagement at the Metropolitan Theatre in Cleveland, Ohio.

Thursday 9 November 1944

Dizzy and Billy Eckstine's Band close at the Metropolitan Theatre in Cleveland, Ohio.

Friday 10 November 1944

Dizzy and Billy Eckstine's Band open a one-week engagement at the Paradise Theatre in Detroit.

Thursday 16 November 1944

Dizzy and Billy Eckstine's Band close at the Paradise Theatre in Detroit.

Sunday 19 November 1944

Dizzy and Billy Eckstine's Band play a dance at the Savoy Ballroom in Chicago.

Saturday 2 December 1944

Dizzy and Billy Eckstine's Band play a dance at the Brooklyn Palace in Brooklyn, New York.

Tuesday 5 December 1944

Billy Eckstine's Orchestra record for Deluxe Records in New York City.

DIZZY GILLESPIE, GAIL BROCKMAN, SHORTY MCCONNELL, MARION HAZEL (trumpets); GERALD VALENTINE, TASWELL BAIRD, HOWARD SCOTT, CHIPS OUTCALT (trombones); JOHN JACKSON, BILL FRAZIER (alto sax); DEXTER GORDON, GENE AMMONS (tenor sax); LEO PARKER (baritone sax); JOHN MALACHI (piano); CONNIE WAINWRIGHT (guitar); TOMMY POTTER (bass); ART BLAKEY (drums); BILLY ECKSTINE, SARAH VAUGHAN (vocal)

If That's The Way You Feel / I Want To Talk About You / Blowing The Blues Away / Opus X / I'll Wait And Pray (vSV) / *The Real Thing Happened To Me*

Friday 8 December 1944

Dizzy and Billy Eckstine's Band open a one-week engagement at the Downtown Theatre in Chicago.

Thursday 14 December 1944

Dizzy and Billy Eckstine's Band close at the Downtown Theatre in Chicago.

Friday 22 December 1944
Dizzy and Billy Eckstine's Band open a one-week engagement at the Apollo Theatre in New York City. Also on the bill are Tip, Tap & Toe, Boyd & Chapman and the Jim Wong Troupe.

Thursday 28 December 1944
Dizzy and Billy Eckstine's Band close at the Apollo Theatre in New York City.

Sunday 31 December 1944
Dizzy records with Sarah Vaughan and her All-Stars for Continental Records in New York City.
DIZZY GILLESPIE (trumpet/piano); AARON SACHS (clarinet); GEORGIE AULD (tenor sax); LEONARD FEATHER (piano); CHUCK WAYNE (guitar); JACK LESBERG (bass); MOREY FELD (drums); SARAH VAUGHAN (vocal)
Signing Off (vSV) / *Interlude* (vSV, p&t DG) / *No Smokes* (vSV, p&t DG) / *East Of The Sun* (vSV, p&t DG)

In the evening, Dizzy and Billy Eckstine's Band play a New Year's Eve dance at the Golden Gate Ballroom in New York.

When the Billy Eckstine Band goes out on the road, Dizzy elects to stay in New York. He has plans for a small bebop combo with Charlie Parker but, in the meantime, busies himself in the recording studios.

Thursday 4 January 1945
Recording session as Clyde Hart's All Stars for Continental in New York City.
DIZZY GILLESPIE (trumpet); CHARLIE PARKER (alto sax); TRUMMY YOUNG (trombone/vocal); DON BYAS (tenor sax); CLYDE HART (piano); MIKE BRYAN (guitar); AL HALL (bass); SPECS POWELL (drums); RUBBERLEGS WILLIAMS (vocal)
What's The Matter Now (vRW) / *I Want Every Bit Of It* (vRW) / *That's The Blues* (vRW) / *G.I. Blues* (vRW) / *4F Blues* (vRW) / *Dream Of You* (vTY) / *Seventh Avenue* (vTY) / *Sorta Kinda* (vTY) / *Oh, Oh, My, My, Oh, Oh* (vTY)

Tuesday 9 January 1945
Dizzy records with his Sextet and a larger group under Oscar Pettiford for Manor Records in New York City.
DIZZY GILLESPIE (trumpet/piano); TRUMMY YOUNG (trombone); DON BYAS (tenor sax); CLYDE HART (piano); OSCAR PETTIFORD (bass); SHELLY MANNE (drums)
I Can't Get Started / *Good Bait* / *Salt Peanuts* / *Be-Bop*
DIZZY GILLESPIE, BILL COLEMAN, BENNY HARRIS, UNKNOWN (trumpets); TRUMMY YOUNG, VIC DICKENSON, BENNY MORTON (trombones); JOHNNY BOTHWELL, UNKNOWN (alto sax); DON BYAS, UNKNOWN (tenor sax); SERGE CHALOFF (baritone sax); CLYDE HART (piano); OSCAR PETTIFORD (bass); SHELLY MANNE (drums); RUBBERLEGS WILLIAMS (vocal)
Something For You / *Worried Life Blues* (vRW) / *Empty Bed Blues Pt1* (vRW) / *Empty Bed Blues Pt2* (vRW)

Friday 12 January 1945
Dizzy Gillespie records with the Joe Marsala Sextet for Black & White Records in New York City.
DIZZY GILLESPIE (trumpet); JOE MARSALA (clarinet); CLIFF JACKSON (piano); CHUCK WAYNE (guitar); IRVING LANG (bass); BUDDY CHRISTIAN (drums)
My Melancholy Baby / *Cherokee* / *Perdido* / *On The Alamo*

Monday 17 January 1945
Dizzy Gillespie records transcriptions with the Boyd Raeburn Orchestra at Liederkrantz Hall in New York City.
DIZZY GILLESPIE, TOMMY ALLISON, STAN FISHELSON, BENNY HARRIS (trumpets); WALTER ROBERTSON (trumpet/trombone); JACK CARMEN, OLLIE WILSON (trombones); JOHNNY BOTHWELL, HAL McKUSICK (alto sax), AL COHN, JOE MEGRO (tenor sax), SERGE CHALOFF (baritone sax); IKE CARPENTER (piano); STEVE JORDAN (guitar); OSCAR PETTIFORD (bass); SHELLY MANNE (drums), DON DARCY (vocal)
Barefoot Boyd With Cheek / *Lonely Serenade* / *Sequence* / *Who's To Answer?* (vDD) / *Blue Moon* / *I'll Always Be In Love With You* / *Summertime* / *Solitude* (vDD) / *Interlude* (vDD)
Esquire magazine announce their pollwinners. Dizzy is voted 'New Star' on trumpet.

Friday 19 January 1945
Dizzy Gillespie is in the Boyd Raeburn Orchestra when it opens a one-week engagement at the Apollo Theatre in New York City.

Thursday 25 January 1945
Dizzy Gillespie and the Boyd Raeburn Orchestra close at the Apollo Theatre in New York City. Dizzy also plays a few one-nighters with the band.

Monday 26 January 1945
Dizzy Gillespie records with the Boyd Raeburn Orchestra for Guild Records in New York City.
DIZZY GILLESPIE, TOMMY ALLISON, STAN FISHELSON, BENNY HARRIS (trumpets); WALTER ROBERTSON (trumpet/trombone); JACK CARMEN, OLLIE WILSON, TRUMMY YOUNG (trombones); JOHNNY BOTHWELL, HAL McKUSICK (alto

sax), AL COHN, JOE MEGRO (tenor sax), SERGE CHALOFF (baritone sax); IKE CARPENTER (piano); STEVE JORDAN (guitar); OSCAR PETTIFORD (bass); SHELLY MANNE (drums)
Night In Tunisia

Tuesday 27 January 1945
Dizzy Gillespie records with the Boyd Raeburn Orchestra for Guild Records in New York City.
DIZZY GILLESPIE, TOMMY ALLISON, STAN FISHELSON, BENNY HARRIS (trumpets); WALTER ROBERTSON (trumpet/trombone); JACK CARMEN, OLLIE WILSON, TRUMMY YOUNG (trombones); JOHNNY BOTHWELL, HAL MCKUSICK (alto sax); AL COHN, JOE MEGRO (tenor sax); SERGE CHALOFF (baritone sax); IKE CARPENTER (piano); STEVE JORDAN (guitar); MICKEY MENDI (bass); SHELLY MANNE (drums); DON DARCY, MARGIE WOOD (vocal)
March Of The Boyds / Prisoner Of Love (vDD) / *I Wanna Get Married* (vMW) / *I Didn't Know About You* (vDD) / *I Promised You* (vDD) / *This Heart Of Mine* (vMW) / *Summertime*

Sunday 4 February 1945
Dizzy Gillespie takes part in a Monte Kay afternoon concert (4–8pm) at the Spotlite Club in New York City. Also appearing are Buck Clayton, Harry Edison, Don Byas, Dexter Gordon, Erroll Garner and Shelly Manne.

Wednesday 7 February 1945
Dizzy Gillespie records with the George Auld Orchestra for Guild Records in New York City.
DIZZY GILLESPIE, BILLY BUTTERFIELD, AL KILLIAN, JIMMY ROMA (trumpets); JOHN D'AGOSTINO, ELI ROBINSON, TRUMMY YOUNG (trombones); GEORGE AULD (alto sax/tenor sax/soprano sax); MUSKY RUFFO, GENE ZANONI (alto sax); AL COHN, AL YOUNG (tenor sax); MANNY ALBAM (baritone sax); ERROLL GARNER (piano); MIKE BRYAN (guitar); CHUBBY JACKSON (bass); SHADOW WILSON (drums); GORDON DRAKE, PATTI POWERS (vocal)
Georgie Porgie / Sweetheart Of My Dreams (vPP) / *I Fall In Love Too Easily* (vGD) / *In The Middle*

Friday 9 February 1945
Dizzy Gillespie Sextet record for Guild Records in New York City.
DIZZY GILLESPIE (trumpet); DEXTER GORDON (tenor sax); FRANK PAPARELLI (piano); CHUCK WAYNE (guitar); MURRAY SHIPINSKI (bass); SHELLY MANNE (drums)
Groovin' High / Blue'n'Boogie

Sunday 11 February 1945
Dizzy Gillespie takes part in a Monte Kay afternoon concert (4–8pm) at the Spotlite Club in New York City. Also appearing are Al Killian, Harry Edison, Eddie Davis, Dexter Gordon, Erroll Garner, Shelly Manne and Buddy Rich.

Monday 19 February 1945
Dizzy Gillespie leads a group at the Witoka Club in Harlem, New York City. Louis Jordan is guest of honor for the evening.

Wednesday 28 February 1945
Recording session as Dizzy Gillespie Sextet for Guild in New York City.
DIZZY GILLESPIE (trumpet); CHARLIE PARKER (alto sax); CLYDE HART (piano); REMO PALMIERI (guitar); SLAM STEWART (bass); COZY COLE (drums)
Groovin' High / All The Things You Are / Dizzy Atmosphere

Monday 19 March 1945
Pianist Clyde Hart dies of tuberculosis aged 35.
Dizzy is a pallbearer at his funeral.

Friday 23 March 1945 (or Wed 28)
Dizzy Gillespie records with the George Auld Orchestra for Guild Records in New York City.
DIZZY GILLESPIE, MANNY FOX, FREDDIE WEBSTER (trumpets); BOBBY ASCHER, GEORGE ARUS, ROGER SMITH (trombones); GEORGE AULD (alto sax/tenor sax/soprano sax); MUSKY RUFFO, GENE ZANONI (alto sax); JOE MEGRO, JACK SCHWARTZ (tenor sax); LARRY MOLINELLI (baritone sax); TONY ALESS (piano); TURK VAN LAKE (guitar); DOC GOLDBERG (bass); IRV KLUGER (drums); PATTI POWERS (vocal)
Lover Man (vPP) / *Co-Pilot / I'll Never Be The Same*

Sunday 25 March 1945
Dizzy Gillespie appears at a Palm Sunday Dance & Jam Session at the Lincoln Square Center in New York City. Also involved are Ben Webster, Tiny Grimes, Cozy Cole, Don Byas, Erroll Garner and others.

Saturday 14 April 1945
Dizzy Gillespie records with Albinia Jones and Don Byas' Swing Seven for National in New York City.
DIZZY GILLESPIE (trumpet); GENE SEDRIC (clarinet); DON BYAS (tenor sax); SAMMY PRICE (piano); LEONARD WARE (guitar); OSCAR SMITH (bass); HAROLD 'DOC' WEST (drums); ALBINIA JONES (vocal)
Evil Gal Blues (vAJ) / *Salty Papa Blues* (vAJ) / *Albinia's Blues* (vAJ) / *Don't Wear No Black* (vAJ)

Sunday 15 April 1945
Dizzy Gillespie and some of his fellow New Star Winners in the 1945 Esquire poll, including Herbie Fields and Aaron Sachs, guest at Lionel Hampton's Concert at Carnegie Hall in New York City.
DIZZY GILLESPIE (trumpet); AL KILLIAN, JOE MORRIS, DAVE PAGE, LAMAR WRIGHT, WENDELL CULLEY (trumpets); ABDUL HAMID, AL HAYSE, JOHN MORRIS, ANDREW PENN (trombones); HERBIE FIELDS (clarinet/alto sax); GUS EVANS (clarinet/alto sax); ARNETT COBB, JAY PETERS (tenor sax); CHARLIE FOWLKES (baritone sax); LIONEL HAMPTON (vibes); MILT BUCKNER (piano); BILLY MACKEL (guitar); CHARLIE HARRIS, TED SINCLAIR (bass); FRED RADCLIFF (drums)
Red Cross

Thursday 26 April 1945

Dizzy Gillespie/Charlie Parker Combo open at the Three Deuces on 52nd Street opposite the Don Byas Band and the Erroll Garner Trio. They are to be resident at the Three Deuces until July.

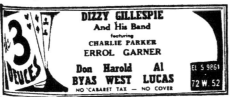

Dizzy Keeps Street Alive

The first big opening on 52nd Street since the curfew took place when Dizzy Gillespie & Co., moved into the Three Deuces. Band features saxophonist Charlie Parker, Al Haig on piano. Drummer is Stan Levey, who held down a similar position with Barney Bigard's small band. Curley Russell is the bass player. Dizzy, winner of the Esquire New Stars trumpet position, until recently was the guiding light of the Billy Eckstine band.

Friday 11 May 1945

Recording session as Dizzy Gillespie and his All Stars for Musicraft in New York City.

DIZZY GILLESPIE (trumpet); CHARLIE PARKER (alto sax); AL HAIG (piano); CURLEY RUSSELL (bass); SIDNEY CATLETT (drums); SARAH VAUGHAN (vocal)

Salt Peanuts (vDG) / *Shaw 'Nuff* / *Lover Man* (vSV) / *Hot House*

Wednesday 16 May 1945

Dizzy Gillespie and Charlie Parker appear at a Town Hall Concert for the New Jazz Foundation. Also billed to appear are Stuff Smith, Georgie Auld, Cozy Cole, Hot Lips Page, Slam Stewart, Dinah Washington, Skippy Williams, Teddy Wilson and the Leonard Feather Trio.

Dizzy Dazzles for an Hour; Rest of Concert Drags

By Barry Ulanov

THE NEW JAZZ FOUNDATION was well-served on Wednesday evening, May 17, at New York's Town Hall, when Dizzy Gillespie made his and the organization's concert debut. Dizzy was in magnificent form; I've never heard him play so well, muff so few notes, and reach such inspired heights. Though nine-tenths of a concert is too much for a small band of the nature of Dizzy's, he and his associates acquitted themselves so well that the superfluity of chromatic runs, daring intervals and triplets, did not get on one's nerves.

The reason Dizzy and Charley Parker (on alto), Al Haig (piano), Curley Russell (bass) and Harold West (drums), had so much to play was that most of the announced guests didn't show. Dinah Washington sang Leonard Feather's E... Blues and Blowtop Blues, ... Leonard at the piano. Dina... as usual, a brilliant shouter, ... best in the delightful lyrics ...

(as in a cadenza), then slamming into tempo, giving his listeners a tremendous release, an excited relief. Al Haig played pleasant piano in Dizzy's groove and Curley and Harold played well; the former with an unusual regard for pitch and a big bass tone; the latter with a good feeling for Dizzy's style, all the more impressive when you realize that he is not his regular drummer.

The second half almost went to pieces. Guests didn't show and Symphony Sid, who was announcing the concert, became flustered and communicated his nervousness to Dizzy and the band. They did well with *Cherokee* and *Blue n' Boogie* and *Dizzy Atmosphere* and *Confirmation*, but not well enough to offset the obvious bewilderment on everybody's face and the long stage waits. And nothing could balance,

Friday 25 May 1945

Recording session as Sarah Vaughan and her Octet for Musicraft in New York City.

DIZZY GILLESPIE (trumpet); CHARLIE PARKER (alto sax); FLIP PHILLIPS (tenor sax); NAT JAFFE, TADD DAMERON (piano); BILL DE ARANGO (guitar); CURLEY RUSSELL (bass); MAX ROACH (drums); SARAH VAUGHAN (vocal)

What More Can A Woman Do? (vSV, pNJ) / *I'd Rather Have A Memory Than A Dream* (vSV, pTD) / *Mean To Me* (vSV, pNJ)

Wednesday 30 May 1945

Dizzy Gillespie and Charlie Parker appear at a Town Hall Concert.

Dizzy also appears in a Memorial Day Benefit Jam Session and Dance at the Lincoln Square Center with Ben Webster, Don Byas, Erroll Garner, Slam Stewart, Mary Lou Wilson and Sid Catlett's All-Star Band.

Tuesday 5 June 1945

Dizzy Gillespie and Charlie Parker appear at a concert at the Academy of Music in Philadelphia. From a recording made at the concert, one number survives:

DIZZY GILLESPIE (trumpet); CHARLIE PARKER (alto sax); AL HAIG (piano); CURLEY RUSSELL (bass); STAN LEVEY (drums)

Blue'n'Boogie

Wednesday 6 June 1945

Recording session as Red Norvo and his Selected Sextet for Comet in New York City.

DIZZY GILLESPIE (trumpet); CHARLIE PARKER (alto sax); FLIP PHILLIPS (tenor sax); RED NORVO (vibes); TEDDY WILSON (piano); SLAM STEWART (bass); SPECS POWELL (drums)

Hallelujah (3 takes) / *Get Happy* (2 takes)

DIZZY GILLESPIE (trumpet); CHARLIE PARKER (alto sax); FLIP PHILLIPS (tenor sax); RED NORVO (vibes); TEDDY WILSON (piano); SLAM STEWART (bass); J.C. HEARD (drums)

Slam Slam Blues (2 takes) / *Congo Blues* (5 takes)

Friday 15 June 1945

Down Beat reviews Dizzy's latest record release:

DIZZY GILLESPIE
Blue'n'Boogie / Groovin' High Guild 1001
Neither side exhibits Dizzy's horn or style to the best advantage. Riffs are not new, except to one who has not dug Dizzy's work before; they're obvious but still interesting. Both sides, except during the ensemble parts, sound a little forced. *Boogie* has piano by Paparelli, under Dizzy's influence, then Dexter Gordon's tenor and Dizzy, typical but far from his best, playing ideas he's played innumerable times before. *Groovin'* showcases Charlie Parker's alto, Slam Stewart on bass and Remo Palmieri on guitar along with Diz's horn, both muted and open.

Friday 22 June 1945

The New Jazz Foundation hold their second and last concert at New York's Town Hall. Dizzy Gillespie Quintet (Dizzy, Charlie Parker, Al Haig, Curley Russell, Max Roach) is featured and Coleman Hawkins is scheduled to play with the Erroll Garner Trio (Al Lucas, Harold West). Also on hand are Slam Stewart, Buck Clayton, Don Byas, Sid Catlett and Pearl Bailey. Symphony Sid Torin is emcee.

Jazz Stars Absence Drag Gillespie Bash

New York—The New Jazz Foundation is still shooting better-than-par. At its latest Town Hall soiree, two of the most widely-heralded stars, Coleman Hawkins and Slam Stewart, didn't show. Me, I'd like to know what goes on here.

If jazz promotors are going to run concerts and charge admission, then, like any other promotor, they must produce what they advertise and must plan their shows if they expect them to click. Several performers with heavy box-office appeal have failed to appear at both NJF shows and jazz fans who forked it good dough to attend the shows must be getting tired of the routine. Apparently contracts aren't made between the promotors and the artists or there wouldn't be such hit-or-miss attendance by announced jazzmen.

Concerts Badly Planned

Furthermore, the concerts are badly planned. This is evident from the confusion existing on stage most of the time, from the meaningless program (rarely does any musician play in order of what he's listed to play), and especially from the stupid emceeing of a local radio announcer named Symphony Sid.

As for the music—well, lot of it was good but too much of it was repetitious and for that reason Dizzy Gillespie's band and Byas certainly offered plenty excitement but how great for so long can they be? Dizzy and man Charlie Parker gave out great music but it would been a big help if their work broken up by other acts instead of being presented in one. Byas played just as well too often, the fault here of being that he had to play missing Hawk's choruses plus own.

Erroll Garner Shines

The only over-worked artist who didn't pall was pianist Erroll Garner. Whether he was playing complex hot jazz with rhythm

NEW JAZZ FOUNDATION
TOWN HALL
123 W. 43rd St., N. Y. C.
Friday Eve., June 22, 8:15 P. M.
presenting
COLEMAN HAWKINS
DIZZY GILLESPIE
Charley Parker   Max Roach
Curley Russell   Al Haig
SLAM STEWART
Pearl   Buck
BAILEY   CLAYTON
Sidney   Don
CATLETT   BYAS
and introducing
ERROLL GARNER
Harold West   Al Lucas
Symphony Sid—Narrator
Tickets on sale at Town Hall and Rainbow Music Shop, 102 W. 125 St., N. Y. C. and Commodore Music Shop, 136 E. 42nd St.

Leonard Feather reports in *Metronome*:

Again, Stars Fail to Appear At Jazz Foundation Concert

The New Jazz Foundation gave its second Town Hall concert on June 22. Announced as an "evening of modern music" and emceed by Symphony Sid of WHOM, it was more varied and in some respects more satisfying than the previous affair, which had consisted of Dizzy Gillespie and only three of the ten promised guest artists.

There were four highlights this time. One was Pearl Bailey, who would highlight anything with her laconic, graceful interpretations of *Fifteen Years*, *Fly Right* and *St. Louis Blues*. It was no surprise to hear from Pearl after the show that her recent MGM screen test was a resounding success.

Erroll Garner, the most venturesome new pianist since Tatum, had the audience spellbound with his solo set. Here is an artist whose future as a concert jazz pianist is assured. His trio set had some brilliant moments, but most of the time he was drowned by Hal West's drumming.

Two servicemen provided the other big kicks of the concert—Sgt. Buck Clayton, playing his exquisitely wistful and tasteful trumpet on three numbers, joined by Don Byas for the last; and Pvt. Tony Sciacca, a talented youngster, in some light, facile clarinet on *Talk of the Town*.

The other stars of the show were Dizzy Gillespie's Quintet, with Big Sid Catlett sitting in for one number, and Don Byas. Dizzy played a disappointing set, taking most of the numbers too fast for comfortable phrasing. Don Byas spoiled his otherwise fine slow numbers by sticking on long, unaccompanied meaningless cadenzas at the end, à la Hawkins, a fad that has become sadly overworked among tenor men.

Main fault of the concert was, as at the previous one, poor organization and production. Pretty soon the NJF will have to live down a reputation for broken promises. It cannot gain prestige until every musician advertised shows up (this time the No. 1 headliner, Coleman Hawkins, was missing), the concert starts on time, the mike works, musicians stop coming on stage obviously high, and the whole thing, in short, lives up to the description "concert." I hope these things can be accomplished, because the NJF's musical ideals are the best.

Below: The hepsations band rehearsing at Nola's Studios.
L to r: Lloyd Buchanan (bass); Max Roach, drums; John Smith, guitar; Al King, Ted kelly, trombones; Harry Pryor, Kenny Dorham, Dizzy, Elmon Wright, Ed Lewis, trumpets; Walter Fuller, arranger; Eddie De Verteuil, Charlie Rouse, Leo Williams, John Walker, Warren Lucky, saxes.

Thursday 5 July 1945
Dizzy Gillespie/Charlie Parker Combo close at the Three Deuces on 52nd Street. Dizzy forms a big band for an 8-week Southern tour with the Nicholas Brothers as 'Hepsations of 1945,' beginning in Virginia on 8 July.

Sunday 8 July 1945

Dizzy Gillespie Orchestra and 'Hepsations of 1945' open their tour at Langley Field in Virginia. Through July and August the tour includes the following venues:

Memorial Auditorium, Raleigh, North Carolina
Auditorium, Roanoke, Virginia
Ball Park & Club, Knoxville, Tennessee
Armory Auditorium, Charlotte, North Carolina
Armory, Danville, Virginia
Armory, Charleston, West Virginia
Asheville, North Carolina
Armory, Durham, North Carolina
Greensboro, North Carolina
Textile Hall, Greenville, North Carolina
Auditorium, Savannah, Georgia
Township Auditorium, Columbia, South Carolina
Riverside Beach Park, Charleston, South Carolina
Southland Palace, Miami, Florida
Jacksonville, Florida
Auditorium, Macon, Georgia
City Auditorium, Atlanta, Georgia
Municipal Auditorium, Birmingham, Alabama
Coliseum Arena, New Orleans, Louisiana
Beaumont, Texas
Galveston, Texas
Houston, Texas
Auditorium, San Antonio, Texas
Fort Worth, Texas
Rose Room, Dallas, Texas
Auditorium, Oklahoma City, Oklahoma (2 days)
Auditorium, Kansas City, Missouri
Auditorium, Topeka, Kansas
Coliseum, Dayton, Ohio
Ezzard Charles Coliseum, Cincinnati, Ohio

Wednesday 1 August 1945

Down Beat reviews Dizzy's latest record release:

DIZZY GILLESPIE
Be-Bop / Salted Peanuts Manor 5000

This could have been thrown out and swing fans would not have missed much. As it is it will undoubtedly give many listeners the wrong impression as to what Dizzy and Charlie Parker and their crew had been putting down on 52nd Street. In the first place, Don Byas, tenor, is on the sides and his horn doesn't blend with Dizzy's nearly as well as Parker's alto. Tone just isn't right for that kind of fast stuff. Then, too, the arrangements are too affected and overdone, so much that it's hardly good swing. Solos are by Dizzy, not too badly done as both solos are long enough to develop some ideas, Don Byas, Trummie Young on trombone, short and uninspired, and the late Clyde Hart on piano. Shelly Manne and Oscar Pettiford provide rhythm, though Shelly sounds a bit bewildered by all the nonsense. This is too frantic to be worthwhile, though noteworthy in being a bit of fresh air in the otherwise too stagnant swing music of today.

Metronome also reviews the record in its August issue:

Dizzy Gillespie
Salted Peanuts A–
Be Bop A–

Standard Gillespie repertoire is brought effectively to wax by the wack himself this month, with fine assistance from Trummy Young, Don Byas, the late Clyde Hart, Oscar Pettiford and Shelly Manne. Dizzy's chromatic descents and ascents, his running triplets, be bops and mops are well served (as anyone who has ever heard him knows) by these two pieces. The *Peanuts* have been put into the past tense by Manor, but they're still the familiar *Salt* (not *Salt-ed*) variety, with Dizzy's crazy vocal (just the title, repeated several times). Don is wonderful on Be Bop, and Dizzy first-rate on both numbers. Surfaces tolerable. (Manor 5000)

Friday 31 August 1945

Dizzy Gillespie and the 'Hepsations of 1945' open a one-week engagement at the McKinley Theatre in thte Bronx, New York City.

Thursday 6 September 1945

Dizzy Gillespie and the 'Hepsations of 1945' close at the McKinley Theatre in the Bronx, New York City.

Saturday 8 September 1945

Dizzy Gillespie takes part in a jam session at the Lincoln Square Center in New York City. Also appearing are Charlie Parker, Don Byas, Stuff Smith, Erroll Garner, Dexter Gordon, Ben Webster, Eddie Barefield and the bands of John Kirby and Duke Ellington.

Sunday 16 September 1945

Dizzy Gillespie takes part in a Monte Kay afternoon concert (4–8pm) at the Spotlite Club in New York City. Also appearing are Al Killian, Don Byas, Charlie Parker, Al Cohn, Al Haig, Leonard Gaskin and Morcy Feld.

Friday 21 September 1945

Dizzy Gillespie Orchestra open a one-week engagement at the Regal Theatre in Chicago.

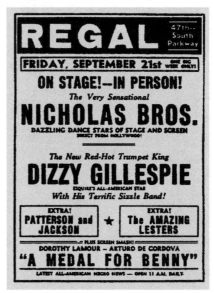

Thursday 27 September 1945
Dizzy Gillespie Orchestra close at Regal Theatre, Chicago.

Friday 28 September 1945
Dizzy Gillespie Orchestra open a one-week engagement at the Paradise Theatre in Detroit.

Thursday 4 October 1945
Dizzy Gillespie Orchestra close at the Paradise Theatre, Detroit. Dizzy breaks up the big band and, to coincide with the release of his Guild recordings, does one-nighters around New York with a small group.

October 1945
Metronome reviews Dizzy's latest Guild releases:

Dizzy Gillespie
Salt Peanuts A–
Hot House A–
Shaw Nuff A
Lover Man B+

Here at last is a session that brings to records an accurate idea of Dizzy's music. The quintet heard here is the same one Diz had at the Three Deuces this summer, except that Sid Catlett is brought in on drums for the records. The alto man, Charlie Parker, and the pianist, young Al Haig, show a striking resemblance to Dizzy in their improvisations.

Shaw Nuff is the most amazing and characteristic performance. The ensemble passages are fast, tricky trumpet-and-alto unison, with unexpected dissonances, harmonic and rhythmic subtleties that are typical of the progressive musical thinking for which Dizzy's crowd stands. *Hot House* is an ingenious variation, by Tad Dameron, based on the chords of *What Is This Thing Called Love*. *Salt Peanuts* is simpler than most Dizzy tunes, but with the same phenomenal solo work by Parker and Dizzy, so frantic that it not only takes your breath away, but their own breath too, with the result that some phrases are left clear in mid-air.

Lover Man is a vocal side featuring Dizzy's and our favorite new singer, Sara Vaughn, but she is hampered by the band, which can't possibly give her the full, rich background needed by her full, rich voice. Dizzy's short solo on this side proves that this kind of tempo and tune is not for him. However, it's a good record, at least worth comparing with the Billie Holiday version. Recording good. (Guild 1003, 1002)

Sunday 21 October 1945
Dizzy Gillespie's 28th birthday. Dizzy rehearses a quintet comprising Charlie Parker, Bud Powell, 19-year-old Ray Brown and Max Roach.

Tuesday 20 November 1945
Dizzy Gillespie takes part in a jazz concert at the Academy of Music in Philadelphia. Also on the bill are Art Tatum, Coleman Hawkins, Mary Osborne, Thelonious Monk, Al McKibbon and Denzil Best. Leonard Feather is emcee.

The show is reviewed by *Metronome*:

Tatum Tops Philly Concert
Academy of Music, Philadelphia

AT PHILLY'S recent jazz concert given at the Academy of Music on November 20, Art Tatum enthralled a large crowd of enthusiasts with his astonishing piano technique, Coleman Hawkins blew good tenor and John "Dizzy" Gillespie displayed his most unusual trumpeting talent. But as good as the Big Three were, this reviewer, and a large number of the jazz fans present, were knocked out more by the gargantuan talent of amazing girl guitarist Mary Osborne.

Apparently dug up at the last minute by emcee Leonard Feather, Mary showed off a fine beat, terrific ideas, a good command of her instrument and an extremely modest personality. Neglected in advance billings, the refugee from Gay Claridge's society outfit was well received by the Philly fans.

Tatum started off the concert and was featured on solo renditions of *Elegie*, *Humoresque* and *Begin the Beguine*. Beautifully done, the first three selections almost bordered on the symphonic. Art hit his stride on *Sweet Lorraine* and concluded the first set with *Danny Boy* and a new version of *Song of the Vagabonds*. The tremendous ovation for Tatum was somewhat marred by the request of an unenlightened army captain. Overcome by Tatum's technique, the captain shouted to Feather, "Can we have the piano turned around so that we can see the keyboard?" I wonder if a good many of the so-called jazz fans present couldn't have been applauding Tatum's fast finger movement rather than his superb artistry.

Hawkins, resplendent in a brown pin-stripe suit, led his Trio on for the next set. Coleman played good if not great tenor in a group of familiar Hawkins specialties. Led by the moving bass work of Al McKibbon and aided by Denzil Best's steady drumming, the trio was hampered not a little by pianist Thelonious Monk.

Gillespie, referred to by Feather as the "Twenty-First Century Gabriel," followed Hawkins and borrowed Bean's Trio. The Diz, goatee and all, maneuvered skilfully through his own *Night in Tunisia*, blew blue on *The Man I Love* and was joined by Hawk on *Groovin' High*. Gillespie, a Philly native son, received a compliment from music reviewer Max de Schauensee of the *Evening Bulletin*. The critic said Diz offered his numbers "with elaborate trumpet cadenza and revealed wonderful smoothness and mastery of his instrument."

After Diz, Tatum returned to offer a smooth medley of tunes by the late Jerome Kern and was followed by Mary Osborne and her guitar. Backed by the Hawkins trio, the guitarist played *Rosetta* and an encore suggested by Feather, *Just You, Just Me*. Obviously unfamiliar with the old standard, Osborne displayed her unusual single-string virtuosity and jazz knowledge. The gal is great and would be a good bet for an enterprising name bandleader in the market for an uncommon commercial asset.

The entire troup, sans Tatum, ended the concert with a resounding *Body and Soul* played for the most part at up tempo. Diz, Hawk and Monk took solos but Miss Mary Osborne, with two exquisite choruses, was the only one to draw a hand from the crowd.

Ably produced, the concert came off well and was not handicapped by Feather's informative commenting. It was a program of modern music unmarred by archaic moldy figgers or unmusical girl vocalists.—DAVE BITTAN

Monday 26 November 1945
Recording session as Charlie Parker's Reboppers for Savoy at the WOR Studios in New York City.
DIZZY GILLESPIE (trumpet/piano); MILES DAVIS (trumpet); CHARLIE PARKER (alto sax); ARGONNE THORNTONAKA SADIK HAKIM (piano); CURLEY RUSSELL (bass); MAX ROACH (drums)
Billie's Bounce (5 takes) / *Warming Up A Riff* / *Now's The Time* (4 takes) / *Thriving On A Riff* (3 takes) / *Meandering* / *Ko-Ko* (2 takes)

Monday 10 December 1945

Dizzy Gillespie and Charlie Parker open at Billy Berg's on Vine Street in Hollywood. Bud Powell and Max Roach are unable to make the California trip and are replaced by Al Haig and Stan Levey. Vibist Milt Jackson is added as insurance against an errant Charlie Parker.

YEAH, CHARLIE PARKER WAS SUCH A GREAT MUSICIAN THAT SOMETIMES HE'D GET LOST AND WOULDN'T SHOW UP UNTIL VERY, VERY LATE. THEN THE GUY WOULD LOOK UP ON THE STAND AND TELL ME, "YOU GOT A CONTRACT FOR FIVE GUYS, AND ONLY FOUR GUYS ON THE STAND, DEDUCT SOME MONEY." SO I HIRED MILT JACKSON AS AN EXTRA MUSICIAN WHEN I WENT TO BILLY BERG'S TO BE SURE THAT WE HAD FIVE MUSICIANS… …THE AUDIENCE WASN'T TOO HIP. THEY DIDN'T KNOW WHAT WE WERE PLAYING… WE WERE ON THE BILL WITH SLIM GAILLARD AND HARRY 'THE HIPSTER' GIBSON, BIG STARS ON THE WEST COAST.

The group record as Dizzy Gillespie and his Rebop Six for the American Armed Forces Radio Services (AFRS) show *Jubilee* which is broadcast weekly to military personnel overseas. The show is produced by Jimmy Lyons.
Dizzy Atmosphere / Groovin' High / Shaw 'Nuff
Dizzy also records *Night in Tunisia* for the show with the Boyd Raeburn Orchestra

Monday 17 December 1945

Dizzy and the group broadcast from Billy Berg's.
DIZZY GILLESPIE (trumpet); CHARLIE PARKER (alto sax); AL HAIG (piano); MILT JACKSON (vibes); RAY BROWN (bass); STAN LEVEY (drums)
I Waited For You / Unknown / 52nd Street Theme / Shaw 'Nuff

Saturday 29 December 1945

Dizzy and Charlie Parker record with Slim Gaillard for Savoy in Los Angeles.
DIZZY GILLESPIE (trumpet); CHARLIE PARKER (alto sax); JACK MCVEA (tenor sax); DODO MARMAROSA (piano); SLIM GAILLARD (guitar, vocal, piano on *Dizzy Boogie*); BAM BROWN (bass); ZUTTY SINGLETON (drums)
Dizzy Boogie (2 takes) / *Flat Foot Floogie* (2 takes) / *Popity Pop* / *Slim's Jam*

1946

Dizzy Gillespie is named Influence of the Year in *Metronome*. He is placed second to Roy Eldridge in the Metronome's annual trumpet poll.

A new company, Paramount Records, set up a date with Dizzy and a string section to record some Jerome Kern music for a memorial album dedicated to the recently deceased composer.
DIZZY GILLESPIE (trumpet); AL HAIG (piano); RAY BROWN (bass); with Johnny Richards' Orchestra
The Way You Look Tonight / Why Do I Love You? / Who / All The Things You Are
After the records are made, Kern's publishers refuse to grant a license for their release on the grounds that Dizzy has departed from the orthodox Kern melodies.

Tuesday 22 January 1946

The first recording session for Dial Records, a new company set up by Ross Russell, owner of the Tempo Music Shop at 5946 Hollywood Boulevard. The plan is to record the Dizzy Gillespie Sextet on its off-night at the club with Lester Young replacing Lucky Thompson (a recent addition to the band at Billy Berg's) with pianist-arranger George Handy supervising and playing piano. When Lester is discovered to have a gig in San Diego, the session is postponed for two weeks.

Thursday 24 January 1946

Dizzy Gillespie and his Rebop Six broadcast over WEAF from Billy Berg's Club in Los Angeles.
DIZZY GILLESPIE (trumpet); CHARLIE PARKER (alto sax); LUCKY THOMPSON (tenor sax); AL HAIG (piano); MILT JACKSON (vibes); RAY BROWN (bass); STAN LEVEY (drums)
Salt Peanuts

Monday 28 January 1946

Dizzy Gillespie and Charlie Parker take part in a *Down Beat* Award Winners Concert at the Philharmonic Hall in Los Angeles. Award winners Charlie Ventura, Willie Smith, Mel Powell and Nat King Cole are featured along with Dizzy, Charlie Parker, Lester Young, Billy Hadnott, Howard McGhee, Al Killian and the Gene Krupa Trio. The concert is staged by Norman Granz. Some of the concert is recorded.
DIZZY GILLESPIE, AL KILLIAN (trumpets); CHARLIE PARKER, WILLIE SMITH (alto sax); CHARLIE VENTURA, LESTER YOUNG (tenor sax); MEL POWELL (piano); BILLY HADNOTT (bass); LEE YOUNG (drums)
Sweet Georgia Brown

And Then I Wrote . . . Dizzy tells Norman Granz, as Mel Powell listens, in his usual quiet, somewhat querulous manner. The scene is backstage at the Los Angeles Philharmonic Auditorium where Granz produced his January 27 jazz concert, featuring, among others, Dizzy and Mel. Others were Willie Smith and Charlie "Bird" Parker, Lester Young and Charlie Venturo, Arnold Ross, Lee Young, Billy Hadnott. Dizzy, at the end of a short (as far as he was concerned it should have been a lot shorter) stay in Hollywood, made a spectacular foray into *The Man I Love* at this concert, with more than able assistance from Lester. Lester has settled in L.A., to the particular delight of hundreds of tenor-men in those parts who imitate his every grunt and groan and tone-less scoop. Mel was in Southern California as featured star with Benny Goodman, the center of other pianists' eager attention and himself the eager bearer of the news that he is going to study with great composer Paul Hindemith this coming Summer. Norman was preparing, at this writing, to wrap up another concert between record album covers, preserving for home listeners the improvisations of performers at the last Philharmonic concert, as he had previous ones in Asch and Philo sets. The latest jazz at the Philharmonic offering of this intense entrepreneur of hot will be made available by Black and White, with whom he has signed a year's contract.—B. U.

Dizzy's Combo Comes Back To New York

New York—Dizzy Gillespie and his combo closes at Billy Berg's in Hollywood February 3 and will head directly east. Gillespie may stop at Chicago for a club date before returning to New York, but following his return here, will build another large band.

Sunday 3 February 1946

Dizzy Gillespie and Charlie Parker close at Billy Berg's on Vine Street in Hollywood.
On the same day, Diz and Bird are privately recorded:
DIZZY GILLESPIE, (trumpet); CHARLIE PARKER (alto sax); LUCKY THOMPSON (tenor sax); UNKNOWN (piano); RED CALLENDER (bass); possibly HAROLD 'DOC' WEST (drums)
Lover Come Back To Me

Monday 4 February 1946

Dizzy Gillespie and Charlie Parker record as the Dizzy Gillespie Jazzmen for Dial at the Electro Broadcasting Studios in Glendale. This first Dial recording date is a fiasco. Lester Young and Milt Jackson fail to show (Lucky Thompson and Arvin Garrison are drafted at the last minute) and the studio is filled with friends and hangers-on. Only one side is salvaged and another session is scheduled for Thursday 7th at 9pm.
DIZZY GILLESPIE, (trumpet); CHARLIE PARKER (alto sax); LUCKY THOMPSON (tenor sax); GEORGE HANDY (piano); ARVIN GARRISON (guitar); RAY BROWN (bass); STAN LEVEY (drums)
Diggin' Diz

Thursday 7 February 1946

The rescheduled recording session by the Dizzy Gillespie Jazzmen for Dial takes place at the Electro Broadcasting Studios in Glendale. This time Charlie Parker fails to show and the 9.00pm session eventually takes place without him.
DIZZY GILLESPIE (trumpet); LUCKY THOMPSON (tenor sax); AL HAIG (piano); MILT JACKSON (vibes); RAY BROWN (bass); STAN LEVEY (drums); THE THREE ANGELS (vocal group)
Diggin' For Diz / Dynamo A / Dynamo B / When I Grow Too Old To Dream (v TTA, 2 takes) / *'Round About Midnight* (2 takes)

Saturday 9 February 1946

Dizzy Gillespie and the rest of the band, excluding Charlie Parker, fly back to New York City.

Wednesday 13 February 1946

Dizzy Gillespie appears at a Concert produced by Nat Segal at the Academy of Music in Philadelphia. Also taking part are Billie Holiday, Al Casey Trio, Buck Clayton, Bud Freeman, Joe Bushkin, John Simmons, Morey Feld and Lee Castle & his Band.

Academy of Music, Philadelphia, February 13.
    Philly's leading jazz impresario, Nat Segall, went all out in his search for talent for his recent production at the Academy of Music and came up with a galaxy of musicians that made for a genuine "all-star" concert. Heading the roster was a Billie Holiday who sang her heart out to the gratification of a good sized crowd... Skipping the intermission, Segal...then sprang his surprise of the evening. The Diz, just in from the Coast on his way to an opening at N.Y.'s Spotlite, did his old friend and former boss a favor by stopping in. He was joined by the Jimmy Golden outfit on a 12-minute *Blues In Boogie*.

Dizzy Gillespie Sextet joins the Coleman Hawkins Quartet for a double-header run at the Spotlite on 52nd Street in New York City. The sextet is Dizzy Gillespie, trumpet; Leo Parker, alto & baritone sax (soon replaced by Sonny Stitt, alto sax); Milt Jackson, vibes; Al Haig, piano; Ray Brown, bass, and Stan Levey, drums.

Friday 22 February 1946

Dizzy Gillespie records for Victor in New York City.
Dizzy Gillespie, (trumpet); Don Byas (tenor sax); Al Haig (piano); Milt Jackson (vibes); Bill De Arango (guitar); Ray Brown (bass); J. C. Heard (drums)
52nd Street Theme / A Night In Tunisia / Ol' Man Rebop / Anthropology (DB out)

Above: Dizzy and J. C. Heard at the February 22 session.

Sunday 3 March 1946

Dizzy Gillespie appears at a Matinee Jam Session at Club 845 in the Bronx, New York City. Don Byas, John Tenny (tenor sax), Buck Clayton, Avery Parrish, Big Sid Catlett and the Tiny Grimes Sextet are also present.

Wednesday 6 March 1946

Dizzy Gillespie (as B. Bopstein) records with Tony Scott's Downbeat Club Septet in New York City.
Dizzy Gillespie (trumpet); Tony Scott (clarinet/alto sax); Ben Webster (tenor sax); Trummy Young (trombone); Jimmy Jones (piano); Gene Ramey (bass); Ed Nicholson (drums); Sarah Vaughan (vocal)
All Too Soon (vSV) / *You're Only Happy When I'm Blue* (vSV) / *Ten Lessons With Timothy*

Clark Monroe, owner of the Spotlite, encourages Dizzy to form a big band to play at the club. Dizzy calls in Walter Fuller to make arrangements and organize the band. Billy Eckstine supplies arrangements, stands, microphones and uniforms from his defunct big band.

Friday 15 March 1946

Dizzy Gillespie begins auditions for his big band at Nola Studios in New York City.

Saturday 13 April 1946

Dizzy Gillespie and his sextet appear in a concert at Town Hall in New York City. Also on the bill are the Slam Stewart Quartet and guitarist Charlie Howard.

dizzy—slam

Town Hall, New York

This concert was presented April 13 by a group of 13 ex-servicemen; it featured 13 musicians and its emcee was born on the 13th. Despite all of which it got a satisfactory, though not packed house, and ran relatively smoothly.

The Townsmen, through spokesman Eddie Gibbs, announced that they plan to present a series of similar concerts of modern, progressive jazz. For their first effort they used Dizzy Gillespie and his sextet from the Spotlite, augmented by alto man Sonny Stitt; Slam Stewart and his quartet; Trummy Young singing and playing with the Dizzy Group; and a new star, guitarist Charlie Howard. Slam opened the concert with a set of five numbers in which the piano of young Billy Taylor and the guitar of recently-ex-Army Johnny Collins competed with the leader's solos. Slam, as usual, vacillated between good music and outright comedy, sometimes combining them.

Dizzy's set was interesting mainly for the work of young Stitt, who sounds and looks amazingly like Charlie Parker and has better execution. But a couple of the numbers were played so fast that intelligent phrasing and clean execution were impossible. Dizzy should watch this and keep his tempos at a point where there can be music instead of just technique.

Trummy was in good form, got a fine hand. Charlie Howard played some interesting guitar, but hammed it up with a little too much grimacing. He was joined by all the musicians for some blues jamming to close the show.

Emcee Leonard Feather, introducing Dizzy, got guffaws with the comment: "I don't think this next artist is a genuine jazz musician. He's not from New Orleans, doesn't use Serutan, and never worked in any 'houses'; and he can read and write." The audience seemed to sympathize with Dizzy's terrible handicaps.

Dizzy Starts Large Outfit

New York—Dizzy Gillespie, doing sensational business at the Spotlite on 52nd street, will augment to 17 men, with a girl singer, and remain there indefinitely. Gillespie started auditions at Nola Studios March 15 and expects to have his band ready in a few weeks.

Wednesday 24 April 1946

Dizzy Gillespie Big Band opens at the Spotlite on 52nd Street in New York City. Coleman Hawkins breaks up his band to join JATP leaving pianist Thelonious Monk free to join Dizzy's big band.

DIZZY GILLESPIE

Dizzy's second attempt to run a big band seems certain to be more successful than his first. Clark Monroe's Spotlite Club has squeezed the 17 men into its limited space, giving them a good chance to whip the ensembles into shape.

It's strange to hear numbers like Be Bop and others featured by the old quintet adapted for the big band. There are some moments of five-trumpet unison that are tremendously exciting. The brass section as a whole is powerful and sensitive in its concerted dynamics, and boasts a brilliant Diz disciple in trumpeter David Burns.

Saxes are led by Sonny Stitt, who's a super Charles Parker, but during Sonny's illness a white boy, Johnny White, is leading. Howard Johnson, who toured Europe with Dizzy in 1937 in the old Teddy Hill band, does some nice Carterish alto work.

Trombonist Slim Moore, tenors Ray Abramson and Warren Lucky contribute good solos. The fine rhythm section has Thelonious Monk, pianist and arranger of some of the best numbers; Ray Brown, featured solo bassist—great; and drummer Kenny Clarke. Vibraharpist Milt Jackson has improved vastly and provides some terrific kicks in solo numbers.

All these and Dizzy too, topped by intriguing modern scores from Tad Dameron, John Lewis and Walter Fuller.—FEATHER.

During the Spotlite engagement Dizzy Gillespie and his Orchestra regularly broadcast from the club. Some of these broadcasts, privately recorded, survive although the exact dates are not known.

DIZZY GILLESPIE, DAVE BURNS, ELMON WRIGHT, TALIB DAWUD, JOHN LYNCH, KENNY DORHAM (trumpets); ALTON MOORE, LEON COMEGYS, CHARLES GREENLEE (trombones); SONNY STITT, HOWARD JOHNSON (alto sax); RAY ABRAMS, WARREN LUCKY (tenor sax); LEO PARKER (baritone sax); THELONIOUS MONK or JOHN LEWIS (piano); MILT JACKSON (vibes); RAY BROWN (bass); KENNY CLARKE (drums)

Things To Come / Second Balcony Jump / Groovin' High / Our Delight / One Bass Hit / Things To Come / Unknown Title / One Bass Hit / I Waited For You / Algo Bueno / Unknown Ballad / Day By Day / The Man I Love / How High The Moon / Unknown Title / Things To Come (theme) / *Shaw 'Nuff / I Waited For You / The Man I Love / Oop Bop Sh'Bam* (vDG) / *'Round About Midnight / Ray's Idea / Cool Breeze / I Waited For You / One Bass Hit / For Hecklers Only / Smokey Hollow Jump / Moody Speaks / Boppin' The Blues*

Wednesday 15 May 1946

Dizzy Gillespie Sextet records for Musicraft in New York City.

DIZZY GILLESPIE, (trumpet/vocal); SONNY STITT (alto sax); AL HAIG (piano); MILT JACKSON (vibes); RAY BROWN (bass); KENNY CLARKE (drums); GIL FULLER, ALICE ROBERTS (vocal)

One Bass Hit / Oop Bop Sh'Bam (vDG, GF) / *A Handfulla Gimme* (vAR) / *That's Earl, Brother*

Above: Dizzy relaxes at the Musicraft recording session. This session marks the very first record date for altoist Sonny Stitt.

Monday 10 June 1946

Dizzy Gillespie and his Orchestra record for Musicraft in New York City.

DIZZY GILLESPIE, DAVE BURNS, RAY ORR, TALIB DAWUD, JOHN LYNCH (trumpets); ALTON MOORE, LEON COMEGYS, CHARLES GREENLEA (trombones); JOHN BROWN, HOWARD JOHNSON (alto sax); RAY ABRAMS, WARREN LUCKY (tenor sax); PEE WEE MOORE (baritone sax); MILT JACKSON (piano); RAY BROWN (bass); KENNY CLARKE (drums); ALICE ROBERTS (vocal)
One Bass Hit I / Our Delight / Good Dues Blues (vAR)

Monday 17 June 1946

Dizzy Gillespie is in a JATP lineup for a concert (8.00pm) in the Carnegie Pop Concerts series at Carnegie Hall in New York City. Also in the lineup are Lester Young, Coleman Hawkins, Illinois Jacquet, Billie Holiday, Buck Clayton, Trummy Young, Kenny Kersey, Al McKibbon and J.C.Heard. Although the concert is a box office success, Dizzy's set does not please *Down Beat* reviewer Mike Levin:

First Group Sour

The first set, played by Jacquet, Allan Eager, J. J. Johnson, Dizzy Gillespie, Ken Kersey, Chubby Jackson, and J. C. Heard struck this writer as being a really unfortunate group. Somehow they didn't get tuned up right, with Eager's tenor, and Dizzy's horn painfully sharp, and nobody's ideas clicking. *Man I Love* was just one of those times when Dizzy couldn't get with it. Sounded as if he were tired and needed rest.

Friday 28 June 1946

Dizzy Gillespie and his Band open a one-week engagement at the Apollo Theatre in New York City. Also on the bill are Thelma Carpenter, Bobby Evans, Moni and Spider Bruce. After the last show, Dizzy and the band double at the Spotlite Club on 52nd Street.

Thursday 4 July 1946

Dizzy Gillespie Orchestra closes at the Apollo Theatre in New York City.

Sunday 7 July 1946

An all-star jam session in Dizzy's honour is held at the Apollo Theatre in New York City. *Above, l to r: Tiny Grimes, Buster Bailey, Gene Ammons, Dizzy, Trummy Young, Slam Stewart and Stuff Smith.*

Monday 8 July 1946

Dizzy Gillespie and his Orchestra play an open-air dance in Colonial Park in New York City.

Tuesday 9 July 1946

Dizzy Gillespie and his Orchestra record for Musicraft in New York City.

DIZZY GILLESPIE, DAVE BURNS, KENNY DORHAM, TALIB DAWUD, JOHN LYNCH, ELMON WRIGHT (trumpets); ALTON MOORE, LEON COMEGYS, GORDON THOMAS (trombones); SONNY STITT, HOWARD JOHNSON (alto sax); RAY ABRAMS, WARREN LUCKY (tenor sax); LEO PARKER (baritone sax); JOHN LEWIS (piano); MILT JACKSON (vibes); RAY BROWN (bass); KENNY CLARKE (drums); ALICE ROBERTS (vocal)
One Bass Hit II / Ray's Idea / Things To Come / He Beeped When He Shoulda Bopped (vAR)

Dizzy Gillespie closes at the Spotlite on 52nd Street in New York City.

Friday 12 July 1946

Dizzy Gillespie Orchestra play a one-nighter in Philadelphia.

Sunday 14 July 1946
Dizzy Gillespie Orchestra play a one-nighter in Monessen, Pennsylvania.

Monday 15 July 1946
Dizzy Gillespie Orchestra play a one-nighter in Toledo, Ohio.

Wednesday 17 July 1946
Dizzy Gillespie Orchestra play a one-nighter in Indianapolis.

Friday 19 July 1946
Dizzy Gillespie Orchestra opens a one-week engagement at the Regal Theatre in Chicago opposite Ella Fitzgerald.

Thursday 25 July 1946
Dizzy Gillespie Orchestra closes at the Regal Theatre in Chicago.

Friday 23 August 1946
Dizzy Gillespie Orchestra opens a one-week engagement at the Riviera Club in St. Louis, Missouri.

Thursday 29 August 1946
Dizzy Gillespie Orchestra closes at the Riviera Club in St. Louis, Missouri.

Saturday 31 August 1946
Dizzy Gillespie Orchestra play a one-nighter in Peoria, Illinois.

Monday 2 September 1946
Dizzy Gillespie Orchestra play a Labor Day Dance at the Savoy Ballroom in Chicago.

Wednesday 25 September 1946
Dizzy Gillespie records with Ray Brown's All Stars for Savoy in New York City.
DIZZY GILLESPIE, DAVE BURNS (trumpets); JOHN BROWN (alto sax); JAMES MOODY (tenor sax); MILT JACKSON (vibes); HANK JONES (piano); RAY BROWN (bass); JOE HARRIS (drums)
For Hecklers Only / Smokey Hollow Jump / Moody Speaks / Boppin' The Blues

Friday 27 September 1946
Dizzy Gillespie Orchestra opens a one-week engagement at the Paradise Theatre in Detroit. Ella Fitzgerald is also on the bill.

Thursday 3 October 1946
Dizzy Gillespie Orchestra closes at the Paradise Theatre in Detroit.

Sunday 13 October 1946
Dizzy Gillespie Orchestra and Sidney Bechet headline 'Jazz Operations' at the Civic Opera House in Chicago. Also on the bill are the Gene Sedric Quintet, George Barnes Sextet, Max Miller Trio, Paul Jordan Octet and the Bud Freeman Quintet.

The Opera House, which seats 3,500 people and was less than two-thirds filled, is not good acoustically for small groups, and much of the sound and a good bit of the enthusiasm of the Paul Jordan and Georgie Barnes groups, Jimmy McPartland and Dizzy Gillespie was lost—perhaps in the 15-story fly above stage.

Bechet's soprano work was actually phenomenal, the several tunes on which he was featured were rousing jazz. Also outstanding in the evening's affair was Gene Sedric's clarinet and tenor sax, particularly on a slow blues original in the first set; Max Miller's trio and Georgie Barnes' sextet. Unhappy was the finish, when Dizzy Gillespie, who was brought all the way in from New York to play practically nothing, and Max Miller tangled in an unfortunate display of personalities. The curtain was brought down while the act was still on.

Friday 18 October 1946

Dizzy Gillespie Orchestra opens a one-week engagement at the Howard Theatre in Washington, D.C. Ella Fitzgerald and Cozy Cole with dancers from 'Carmen Jones' are also on the bill.

Monday 21 October 1946

Dizzy Gillespie's 29th birthday.

Thursday 24 October 1946

Dizzy Gillespie Orchestra closes at the Howard Theatre in Washington, D.C.

Friday 25 October 1946

Dizzy Gillespie Orchestra opens a one-week engagement at the Royal Theatre in Baltimore. Ella Fitzgerald and Cozy Cole with dancers from 'Carmen Jones' are also on the bill.

Thursday 31 October 1946

Dizzy Gillespie Orchestra closes at the Royal Theatre in Baltimore.

November 1946

Metronome reviews Dizzy's latest Musicraft release:

Dizzy Gillespie

One Bass Hit (Parts 1 & 2)

This is two parts of part one, because there ain't no part two. The two sides are the same thing, with the sextet playing on the first and then the full band echoing on the reverse, all the trumpets playing like Dizzy where Dizzy had soloed. A good portion of both sides is taken up by Ray Brown's good but under-recorded bass. The first is more authentic be-bop, the second is cuter and has poorer time. Don't judge Dizzy's new band by this. (Musicraft 404)

Saturday 2 November 1946

Dizzy Gillespie and his Orchestra and Ella Fitzgerald play a one-nighter at the Palais Royal Ballroom in Norfolk, Virginia.

Monday 4 November 1946

Dizzy Gillespie and his Orchestra and Ella Fitzgerald open a two-night engagement at the Booker T Theatre in Norfolk, Virginia.

Tuesday 5 November 1946

Dizzy Gillespie and his Orchestra and Ella Fitzgerald close at the Booker T Theatre in Norfolk, Virginia.

Tuesday 12 November 1946

Dizzy Gillespie and his Orchestra record for Musicraft in New York City.

DIZZY GILLESPIE, DAVE BURNS, MATTHEW MCKAY, JOHN LYNCH, ELMON WRIGHT (trumpets); ALTON MOORE, TASWELL BAIRD, GORDON THOMAS (trombones); JOHN BROWN, SCOOPS CARRY (alto sax); JAMES MOODY, BILL FRAZIER (tenor sax); PEE WEE MOORE (baritone sax); JOHN LEWIS (piano); MILT JACKSON (vibes); RAY BROWN (bass); JOE HARRIS (drums); KENNY HAGOOD (vocal)

I Waited For You (vKH) / *Emanon*

Sunday 17 November 1946

Dizzy Gillespie Orchestra and Ella Fitzgerald play a dance at the Savoy Ballroom in Chicago.

December 1946

Metronome reviews Dizzy's latest Musicraft release:

Dizzy Gillespie

Good Dues Blues
Our Delight ★

Both sides by the big band. The blues, slow, starts with Ellington *Bakiff* riffing, goes into a vocal by Alice Roberts. She sings like a deeper Dinah Washington, but with less consistent pitch. The bebop backgrounds, though cute, destroy the blues mood. Dizzy's band was not meant for this kind of performance. Dizzy plays a few good bars in the last chorus. *Delight* is much closer to the spirit of the band. A Tad Dameron original starting out like *If Dreams Come True*, it's well scored, with nice sax and trombone section work backed by strong rhythm. Dizzy sounds relaxed and composed on his solos. There's some good tenor (Ray Abramson?). A good side, though still not the band at its best. (Musicraft 399)

Tuesday 10 December 1946

Ella Fitzgerald and the Dizzy Gillespie Orchestra play a one-nighter at the Dorie Miller Auditorium in Austin, Texas.

Wednesday 11 December 1946
Ella Fitzgerald and the Dizzy Gillespie Orchestra play a one-nighter in Houston, Texas.

Thursday 12 December 1946
Ella Fitzgerald and the Dizzy Gillespie Orchestra open a two-nighter in San Antonio, Texas.

Friday 13 December 1946
Ella Fitzgerald and the Dizzy Gillespie Orchestra close in San Antonio, Texas.

Saturday 14 December 1946
Ella Fitzgerald and the Dizzy Gillespie Orchestra play a one-nighter in Austin, Texas.

Sunday 15 December 1946
Ella Fitzgerald and the Dizzy Gillespie Orchestra play a one-nighter in San Antonio, Texas.

Tuesday 17 December 1946
Ella Fitzgerald and the Dizzy Gillespie Orchestra play a one-nighter in Little Rock, Arkansas.

Wednesday 18 December 1946
Ella Fitzgerald and the Dizzy Gillespie Orchestra play a one-nighter in Ruston, Louisiana.

Thursday 19 December 1946
Ella Fitzgerald and the Dizzy Gillespie Orchestra play a one-nighter in Galveston, Texas.

Friday 20 December 1946
Ella Fitzgerald and the Dizzy Gillespie Orchestra play a one-nighter in Alexandria, Louisiana.

Wednesday 25 December 1946
Ella Fitzgerald and the Dizzy Gillespie Orchestra play a one-nighter in Jackson, Mississippi.

Thursday 26 December 1946
Ella Fitzgerald and the Dizzy Gillespie Orchestra play a one-nighter in Memphis, Tennessee.

Friday 27 December 1946
Ella Fitzgerald and the Dizzy Gillespie Orchestra play a one-nighter in Birmingham, Alabama.

Saturday 28 December 1946
Ella Fitzgerald and the Dizzy Gillespie Orchestra play a one-nighter in Nashville, Tennessee.

Monday 30 December 1946
Ella Fitzgerald and the Dizzy Gillespie Orchestra play a one-nighter in Atlanta, Georgia.

Tuesday 31 December 1946
Ella Fitzgerald and the Dizzy Gillespie Orchestra play a one-nighter in Meridian, Mississippi.

1947

Wednesday 1 January 1947
Ella Fitzgerald and the Dizzy Gillespie Orchestra play a one-nighter in New Orleans. Dizzy is voted top trumpet of 1946 in the *Metronome* poll and is featured in the magazine's Blindfold Test conducted by Leonard Feather.

Thursday 2 January 1947
Ella Fitzgerald and the Dizzy Gillespie Orchestra play a one-nighter in Gulfport, Mississippi.

Friday 3 January 1947
Ella Fitzgerald and the Dizzy Gillespie Orchestra play a one-nighter in Pensacola, Florida.

Saturday 4 January 1947
Ella Fitzgerald and the Dizzy Gillespie Orchestra play a one-nighter in Tuskegee, Alabama.

Wednesday 15 January 1947
Down Beat reviews Dizzy Gillespie's latest Musicraft releases.

Dizzy Gillespie
*** *Oop Bop Sh'Bam*
*** *That's Earl, Brother*
** *Our Delight*
** *Good Dues Blues*

First two are with Diz' small band, second with the large. On *Bam*, he plays two six bar ideas that justify the two clinkers he makes. *Earl's* tempo starts out a little uncertainly. There is a shift from unison to part writing during the middle of a phrase transition that will surprise you. I still want to hear some better tone from all concerned, from Dizzy on down.

Our Delight, scored by Tad Dameron, has a feel and sound similar to Donahue at the inception. The recording doesn't convey the awe-ful smack this band can have when it is really swinging. Dizzy sounds sure of what he's doing but the brass feels a little worried. Alice Roberts' vocaling on the blues sounded shallow and uncertain. Be-bopping back of her is contrasting, but it must be murder for a singer to work against. (*Musicaft 383, 399*)

Friday 17 January 1947
Dizzy Gillespie Orchestra open a one-week engagement at the Apollo Theatre, New York City. Also on the bill are Sarah Vaughan, Lora Pierre, The Edwards Brothers, Jackie 'Moms' Mabley, Stepin Fetchit and Mantan Moreland.

Wednesday 22 January 1947

Dizzy Gillespie Orchestra broadcast from the Apollo Theatre in New York City.

DIZZY GILLESPIE, DAVE BURNS, MATTHEW MCKAY, JOHN LYNCH, ELMON WRIGHT (trumpets); ALTON MOORE, TASWELL BAIRD, GORDON THOMAS (trombones); JOHN BROWN, SCOOPS CARRY (alto sax); JAMES MOODY, BILL FRAZIER (tenor sax); PEE WEE MOORE (baritone sax); JOHN LEWIS (piano); MILT JACKSON (vibes); RAY BROWN (bass); JOE HARRIS (drums)
Lady Bird

Thursday 23 January 1947

Dizzy Gillespie Orchestra close at Apollo Theatre, New York City. It is possibly during the Apollo engagement that Dizzy and the band make a 60-minute musical film called 'Jivin' In Bebop,' which also features Helen Humes. The tunes recorded for the soundtrack are: *Salt Peanuts* (vDG) / *Be-Baba-Le-Ba* (vHH) / *Oop Bop Sh'Bam* (vDG) / *Dizzy's Untitled Original* / *Shaw 'Nuff* / *I Waited For You* (vKH) / *Night In Tunisia* / *Crazy 'Bout A Man* (vHH) / *One Bass Hit* / *Dynamo A* / *Ornithology* / *He Beeped When He Shoulda Bopped* (vDG) / *Droppin' A Square* / *Things To Come* / *Ray's Idea* / *Bags' Boogie*

Friday 24 January 1947

Dizzy Gillespie Orchestra play a one-nighter at the Mercantile Hall in Philadelphia.

Saturday 25 January 1947

Dizzy Gillespie Orchestra play a one-nighter in Atlantic City.

Friday 7 February 1947

Dizzy Gillespie Orchestra play a one-nighter in Westchester, Pennsylvania.

Saturday 8 February 1947

Dizzy Gillespie Orchestra play a one-nighter in Newark, New Jersey.

Dizzy attends the Louis Armstrong matinée concert (5.30pm) at Carnegie Hall in New York City.

Dizzy visits Louis Armstrong backstage at Carnegie Hall.

Wednesday 12 February 1947

Dizzy Gillespie Orchestra play a one-nighter in Cincinnati, Ohio.

Down Beat reviews Dizzy Gillespie's latest Musicraft release.

Dizzy Gillespie
*** *Emanon*
*** *Things To Come*

Recorded in late '46, *Emanon* is the best attempt yet to catch the "whomp" of the big Gillespie band on wax. Unfortunately it doesn't quite come off, though there are some good strings of Dizzy phrases played by himself and the four Dizzyites in the trumpet section. Balance is muddy, and the band's reading isn't as clean as it should be and has been in person. *Things* is one of the wildest arranged sides you will ever hear. Dizzy used to use it to close his *Spotlite* Club shows, but it was much more effective then simply because it was played better. Milt Jackson's vibes still are ideaful but bad-toned. Dizzy himself playing excellently. Small gold cup to Ray Brown for keeping a bass beat going through all the weirdings. (*Musicraft 447*)

Metronome also reviews the record:

Dizzy Gillespie

Things To Come B+
Emanon B+

It's wild, man! It's frantic! It's Dizzy! *Things To Come*, which had better not be an augury of anything if brassmen are going to hold on to their lips, is taken at the uppest up-tempo ever, and still retains grooves full of fine music, paraded by Dizzy, Milt Jackson on vibes, Porter Kilbert on alto and Walter Fuller's nimble scoring. Reverse is *No Name* reversed (get it?), but the music is not, therefore, a series of inversions. It's typical Be-Bop (if there is such a thing), with more of Dizzy's horn, the Jackson vibraphone (which needs welding or reupholstering or something), brisk and fresh piano and Dizzy's own writing, peaked by some high-register unison figures for the whole trumpet section. These are what might be called "A" arrangements; but the ragged ensembles on both sides cut the ratings down. (Musicraft 447)

Friday 14 February 1947

Dizzy Gillespie Orchestra open at the Paradise Theatre, Detroit for a one-week engagement opposite the Illinois Jacquet Orchestra.

…It took 15 mounted cops two hours to quell an outside riot at the Paradise theater in Detroit, when patrons inside continued to dig Dizzy Gillespie and wouldn't leave.

Thursday 20 February 1947

Dizzy Gillespie Orchestra close at the Paradise Theatre, Detroit.

Saturday 22 February 1947

Dizzy Gillespie Orchestra play a one-nighter in Dayton, Ohio.

Sunday 23 February 1947

Dizzy Gillespie Orchestra play a one-nighter in Buffalo, New York.

Wednesday 26 February 1947

Dizzy Gillespie Orchestra open at the Savoy Ballroom in New York City.

Saturday 15 March 1947

Dizzy Gillespie is among the guests at a Lionel Hampton Concert (11.30pm) at Carnegie Hall in New York City. Other guests include Ella Fitzgerald, Count Basie, the Ink Spots, Billy Eckstine and Cootie Williams.

Saturday 22 March 1947

Dizzy Gillespie appears on WNEW's 'Saturday Night Swing Session' with Ella Fitzgerald and Count Basie.

Tuesday 8 April 1947

Charlie Parker, newly arrived in New York from Los Angeles, sits in with the Dizzy Gillespie Orchestra at the Savoy Ballroom in New York City.

Friday 11 April 1947

Dizzy Gillespie Orchestra close at the Savoy Ballroom in New York City.

Thursday 17 April 1947

Dizzy Gillespie Orchestra play a one-nighter in Baltimore, Maryland.

Friday 18 April 1947

Dizzy Gillespie Orchestra open a three-day engagement at the Music Hall in Washington, D.C.

Sunday 20 April 1947

Dizzy Gillespie Orchestra close at the Music Hall in Washington, D.C.

Monday 21 April 1947

Dizzy Gillespie's rhythm section, Milt Jackson, John Lewis, Ray Brown and Teddy Stewart, appear with tenorist James Moody at a Blue Monday Jam Session at Smalls Paradise in Harlem, New York City.

Wednesday 23 April 1947

Down Beat reviews Dizzy Gillespie's new album released by Musicraft.

Dizzy Gillespie Sextet

*** *Groovin' High*
** *A Handful Of Gimme*
*** *Hot House*
** *Blue'N Boogie*
** *Ray's Idea*
** *He Beeped When He Shoulda Bopped*
*** *All The Things You Are*
*** *Dizzy Atmosphere*

This one makes an interesting album. Three of the sides were cut about six months ago (*Gimme, Idea*, and *Beeped*), while the rest are old sides cut for the Guild label and issued here.

Listen carefully and you will hear a marked change in the playing of the musicians around Dizzy, and a constant shift towards more extreme forms of the style labeled be bop.

Groovin' uses almost conventional rhythm section work (Remo Palmieri—guitar, Harold West—drums, Clyde Hart—piano, and Slam Stewart—bass) with a Charlie Parker alto solo of superb fluidity and in-tune Dizzy, while *Gimme* is a blues vocal by Alice Roberts with the now more conventional implied double-time effects and stop beats in the rhythm. Bass is under-balanced, and la Roberts is *very* much out of tune.

Hot House, a Tad Dameron idea, is somewhat mushily played, again with fine alto by Parker. These sides should show you what all the raving has been about as opposed to some of the tripe he turned out before his sickness. Gillespie's solo has a parcel of good ideas, while the final unison figures are more cleanly played.

Blue'N Boogie's piano solo is slightly shaky, and the Dexter Gordon tenor strained. Dizzy himself is not too successful. *Ray* is a big band disc, with a lot of sock but a very wobbly trombone chorus to sink the middle. *Beeped* was the subject of much argument with Leeds Music, as to whether it was bought or not. Alice Roberts' vocal is so bad as to cause wonder how she got on the date, and why the tune's ownership should be too controversial.

Things is tasty, with Gillespie and Parker both playing in good taste and the Slam Stewart bass useful for rhythm if not its usual solo. *Atmosphere* sports more Parker and better Stewart bass.

Here at least the "older" sides top the new—two years go by and already you start talking about an "older" style. How fast can you get! At any rate, if you are one of those sorely puzzled by be bop, and count it as noisy trash, hear *Groovin'* several times—it may be an easier come-on than some of Dizzy's later records. (*Musicraft* 485, 486, 487, 488)

Thursday 24 April 1947
Dizzy Gillespie Orchestra play a one-nighter in Jersey City, New Jersey.

Friday 25 April 1947
Dizzy Gillespie Orchestra play a one-nighter in Newark, New Jersey.

Dizzy Plays For Dance Recital

New York—Tie-in between jazz and the dance has become pronounced in these parts. On May 7, Dizzy Gillespie will accompany Asadata Dafora in a dance recital sponsored by the African Academy of Arts and Research. Affair will be held at the Hotel Diplomat.

On April 16, dancer Mura Dehn used Art Hodes orchestra for support. The reviews, incidentally, aimed all their raves at the musical accompanists.

Wednesday 7 May 1947
Dizzy Gillespie accompanies Asadata Dafora in a dance recital sponsored by the African Academy of Arts and Research at the Hotel Diplomat in New York City.

Monday 12 May 1947
Dizzy Gillespie takes part in a JATP Carnegie Pops Concert at Carnegie Hall in New York City.

Trumpet Men Concert Stars

New York—Second of the Granz Jazz at the Philharmonic concerts during the Carnegie Hall Pop season here spotlighted a session with trumpet players Dizzy Gillespie and Roy Eldridge. Both played well on *Lady Be Good*, with everyone noting a marked improvement in Little Jazz's playing over recent months. Evidently the trouble Roy has had with his teeth is over and he is settling down again. Gillespie's work was better-toned and more restrained than usual. Coleman Hawkins, blowing during the same set, forced the two trumpet men to play well by a magnificent *Yesterdays* incorporating his own tenor style with the constant implied double-timings used by current younger musicians.

Other high-lights were the consistently able piano support of Hank Jones, Willie Smith's lush but powerful altoing of *Sophisticated Lady* and the fantastically powerful drumming of Buddy Rich. His flashiness, power-to-spare and showmanship have yet to be equaled according to the audience, this writer and other concert-drummer, Alvin Stoller.
—*mix*

Well, Be-Bop!

(Staff Photo by Got)

New York—This study of Dizzy Gillespie is from the camera of staffer Bill Gottlieb, depicting the be-bopper's characteristic hat, spectacles, horn, goatee and slouch.

Thursday 15 May 1947
Dizzy Gillespie Orchestra play a Battle of Swing with Illinois Jacquet and his Orchestra at Westchester County Center in White Plains, New York.

Friday 16 May 1947
Dizzy Gillespie Orchestra play a one-nighter in New Haven, Connecticut.

Wednesday 21 May 1947
Dizzy Gillespie Orchestra play a one-nighter in Jersey City, New Jersey.

Friday 23 May 1947
Dizzy Gillespie Orchestra play a one-nighter in Brooklyn, New York City.

Be Bop Music To Be Featured At UNAVA's Town Hall Program

Jazz in the modern idiom will be heard at Town Hall on May 31 when Dizzy Gillespie and Charlie Parker, the two most famous exponents of the be-bop music will demonstrate the new style of jazz.

Trumpeter Gillespie, and alto saxophonist Charlie Parker will be backed up by a quartet drawn from Gillespie's band that will include Ray Brown, bassist, and Milt Jackson, vibraharpist, both 1947 Esquire Magazine New Star Award Winners.

Occasion will be 'Salute to Negro Veterans,' a program dedicated to the role of Negro troops in World War II. The affair is sponsored by the United Negro and Allied Veterans of America, and will present in addition to the above musicians, Dan Burley, managing editor of the New York Amsterdam News who will play piano blues; Muriel Gaines, Hope Foye and the Harlem Symphonic Choir.

Saturday 31 May 1947
Dizzy Gillespie and Charlie Parker take part in the 'Salute to Negro Veterans' concert at Town Hall in New York City.

Town Hall Concert Salutes Negro Vets
New York—In a salute to 1,154,000 Negro war veterans, the United Negro and Allied veterans of America conducted a special program at Town Hall, May 31, that featured Dizzy Gillespie and Charlie (Yardbird) Parker in their first joint effort since Parker returned from the coast.

Diz Inks Victor Pact
New York — Dizzy Gillespie, recently departed from Musicraft, signed a fat one with Victor early this month. Contract calls for eight sides and four cent royalties the first year, ten sides and five cent royalties second year. Diz stands to get over $2,000 each session.

Dizzy is currently working on a Sept. 29 Carnegie hall concert. Rehearsals include rhumba rhythm sections which will be used in two concertos, *Cubanabop* and *Cubanabeep*. Both pieces and another called *Soulphony*, were written by Tad Dameron. Should the concert click, Diz will take the concert on the road.

Gillespie At New Detroit Spot
Detroit—The new Club El Sino has been doing good business with Andy Kirk and, currently, Dizzy Gillespie. With other spots

Friday 6 June 1947
Dizzy Gillespie Orchestra open a two-week engagement at El Sino in Detroit, Michigan.

Thursday 19 June 1947
Dizzy Gillespie Orchestra close at El Sino in Detroit, Michigan.

Friday 20 June 1947
Dizzy Gillespie Orchestra open a one-week engagement at the Apollo Theatre, New York City. Also on the bill are Sarah Vaughan, the Four Step Brothers and Nick & Anita Ball.

Thursday 26 June 1947
Dizzy Gillespie Orchestra close at Apollo Theatre, New York City.

Friday 27 June 1947

Dizzy Gillespie Orchestra open a one-week engagement at the Howard Theatre in Washington, D.C.

Thursday 3 July 1947

Dizzy Gillespie Orchestra close at the Howard Theatre in Washington, D.C.

Thursday 10 July 1947

Dizzy Gillespie Orchestra opens at the Downbeat Club on 52nd Street in New York City. The Barbara Carroll Trio are also on the bill.

Below: Charlie Parker drops into the Downbeat between sets at the Three Deuces to hear Dizzy who is reflected in the mirror with bassist Clyde Lombardi and pianist Barbara Carroll. Sitting next to Parker is Red Rodney who is working nearby at the Troubadour with Georgie Auld's Band. Bottom: 52nd Street at this time. Charlie Parker and his Quintet joined Coleman Hawkins on the bill at the Three Deuces on August 7th.

WE ARE PROUD TO PRESENT
The King of Modern Music
DIZZY GILLESPIE
•
BARBARA CARROLL TRIO
•
DANCING — NO COVER
AIR-CONDITIONED
CLUB
Downbeat
66 W. 52nd   EL. 5-8773

Barry Ulanov reviews the band for *Metronome*:

Dizzy Gillespie
in spite of some lapses, 'clearly the most interesting band around right now'

Dizzy Gillespie's personnel: Trumpets: Dizzy Gillespie, Dave Burns, Elmon Wright, Raymond Orr, Matthew McKay. Trombones: Taswell Baird, William Shepherd. Saxes: Howard Johnson, John Brown, Joe Gayles, James Moody, Cecil Payne. Piano: John Lewis. Bass: Ray Brown. Drums: Joe Harris. Vibes: Milt Jackson. Vocals: Kenneth Hagood, Dizzy Gillespie.

DIZZY'S new band, if you are of anything like my jazz persuasion, will alternately delight and provoke you. You will dape with astonishment at its best moments and shake your head with annoyance at its worst and wonder why it can't be as good as it is some of the time all of the time. But for all your annoyance and wonder you will (if, I repeat, you think the way I do) recognize that it is clearly the most interesting band around right now and you will congratulate Dizzy for having it and yourself for recognizing it.

There is much to be annoyed with: the rough entrances, after all these performances, in *Things To Come*; the shameless illinoises of James Moody's tenoring; the endless quotations of trivia, with a curious emphasis on the songs celebrating Christmas, *Jingle Bells* and *Santa Claus Is Coming To Town*; the clumsy productions with which Milt Jackson's vibraphone solos are surrounded, more in the spirit of motion picture jazz than bebop; the senseless screams (vocal, not instrumental) by the band in a body, in aimless imitation of Lionel Hampton's hollerers. But there is even more, for me at least, to be pleased with: Dizzy's solos, which sometimes, after a cadenza introduction, approach the furious brilliance of his recorded *Congo Blues* effort; the streams of unison trumpet team up-beats in double-time; Cecil Payne's fluent, well-structured baritone contributions; Ray Brown's loose, fresh, mussicianly bass-playing (when he isn't wasting time in parodying Slam Stewart's novelty bowings); the bulk of exciting manuscript, most of it old but most of it good, with which the band is provided; Kenneth "Pancho" Hagood's singing, better all the time, more controlled, less ridden by a wild vibrato and tastefully influenced by Sarah Vaughan and Billy Eckstine.

I would prefer to hear Dizzy with a small band; I think he does his best work with one; I know he has to waste less time in rehearsal and consequently can spend more shaping his ideas, giving his musical utterances fresher, firmer form. But I would rather hear Dizzy with any band than not hear him at all and there is a lot to hear in any band he leads. He is well aware of the shortcomings of this present outfit; he will overcome many of them when time and tide and Victor records provide him with the necessary gold. Perhaps he will find "some more cats like Cecil Payne" in Brooklyn, where he discovered the excellent baritone man and "an alto who blew me right out of the room; I wish I remembered his name…"

Money and the scarcity of first-rate musicians, men capable of playing at Dizzy's level, explain some of the band's limitations. Another is due to a psychological or philosophical quirk (depending upon your point of view). Those quotes. Listen, for example, to Dizzy's lovely coda to *I Can't Get Started* and then hold yourself in readiness for a disappointing wry twist at the end, a sour interpolation of *Jingle Bells*, which twists and tears the preceding loveliness to pieces. The reason, I think, is most obvious: Dizzy, like most of his colleagues and imitators, is afraid to commit himself to any musical statement bordering on the exalted; his personal philosophy is a bitter one and that bitterness rips through much of what he does. Now, don't mistake me; I don't mean to censure him for avoiding the banal prettiness of the popular song melody; and I appreciate a good deal of his acrid musical comment — it's generally refreshing, vigorous, in virile contrast to the pantywaist admirers of the lush tune and syrupy treatment who crowd most of the meaning out of jazz. But bitterness makes a poor staple for any diet, musical or otherwise, and Dizzy would do well to give this as well as the over-frantic clowning, which proceeds from the bitterness, more than casual thought. For John Birks Gillespie is a serious musician at heart, and a well-equipped one, and it's as such that we rate him so highly and want to continue to regard him.

Some privately recorded broadcasts from the Downbeat engagement survive: *I Waited For You* (theme) / *Groovin' High* / *Oop-Pop-A-Da* (vDG, KH) / *Cool Breeze* / *Stay On It* / *Lady Bird*
I Waited For You (theme) / *Woody'n You* / *Two Bass Hit* / *Oop-Bop-Sh'Bam* (vDG, KH) / *Hot House* / *Ray's Idea* / *Pan-Dameronia*

Friday 22 August 1947
Dizzy Gillespie and his Orchestra record for Victor in New York City.
DIZZY GILLESPIE, DAVE BURNS, MATTHEW MCKAY, RAY ORR, ELMON WRIGHT (trumpets); TED KELLY, BILL SHEPHERD (trombones); JOHN BROWN, HOWARD JOHNSON (alto sax); JAMES MOODY, JOE GAYLES (tenor sax); CECIL PAYNE (baritone sax); JOHN LEWIS (piano); MILT JACKSON (vibes); AL MCKIBBON (bass); JOE HARRIS (drums); KENNY HAGOOD (vocal)
Ow! / *Oop-Pop-A-Da* (vDG, KH) / *Two Bass Hit* / *Stay On It*

Sunday 24 August 1947
Dizzy Gillespie, Charlie Parker and Max Roach appear on the Weekly Coffee Hour at the Harlem Servicemen's Center in New York City.

Thursday 28 August 1947
Dizzy Gillespie Orchestra close at the Downbeat Club in New York City.

Sunday 31 August 1947
Dizzy Gillespie Orchestra play a dance at Park City Bowl, 63rd and South Parkway, Chicago.

Saturday 13 September 1947

Dizzy Gillespie plays with Barry Ulanov's All Star Modern Jazz Musicians on the 'Bands for Bonds' radio broadcast via station WOR from the Mutual Studios in New York City. The show is compered by Barry Ulanov, Bruce Elliot and Rudy Blesh.

CHARLIE PARKER (alto sax); DIZZY GILLESPIE (trumpet); JOHN LA PORTA (clarinet); LENNIE TRISTANO (piano); BILLY BAUER (guitar); RAY BROWN (bass); MAX ROACH (drums)

Koko (theme) / *Hot House* / *Fine And Dandy* / *I Surrender Dear* (CP out)

Saturday 20 September 1947

Dizzy Gillespie again plays with Barry Ulanov's All Star Modern Jazz Musicians on the 'Bands for Bonds' radio broadcast via station WOR from the Mutual Studios in New York City. The show is compered by Barry Ulanov, Carl Caruso and Rudy Blesh.

CHARLIE PARKER (alto sax); DIZZY GILLESPIE (trumpet); JOHN LA PORTA (clarinet); LENNIE TRISTANO (piano); BILLY BAUER (guitar); RAY BROWN (bass); MAX ROACH (drums)

Koko (theme) / *On The Sunny Side Of The Street* / *52nd Street Theme* / *Tiger Rag—Dizzy Atmosphere* / *How Deep Is The Ocean?*

Thursday 25 September 1947

Dizzy Gillespie Big Band close a short engagement at the Savoy Ballroom in New York City.

Monday 29 September 1947

Dizzy Gillespie Big Band with Ella Fitzgerald star in a concert at Carnegie Hall in New York City. Charlie Parker appears as a guest star. Cuban drummer Chano Pozo debuts with the band on *Cubana Be-Cubana Bop*.

CHARLIE PARKER (alto sax); DIZZY GILLESPIE (trumpet); JOHN LEWIS (piano); AL MCKIBBON (bass); JOE HARRIS (drums)

A Night In Tunisia / *Dizzy Atmosphere* / *Groovin' High* / *Confirmation* / *Koko*

DIZZY GILLESPIE, DAVE BURNS, MATTHEW MCKAY, RAY ORR, ELMON WRIGHT (trumpets); TASWELL BAIRD, BILL SHEPHERD (trombones); JOHN BROWN, HOWARD JOHNSON (alto sax); JAMES MOODY, JOE GAYLES (tenor sax); CECIL PAYNE (baritone sax); JOHN LEWIS (piano); MILT JACKSON (vibes); AL MCKIBBON (bass); JOE HARRIS (drums); KENNY HAGOOD (vocal)

Cool Breeze / *Relaxin' At Camarillo* / *One Bass Hit* / *The Nearness Of You* / *Salt Peanuts* (vDG) / *Cubana Be-Cubana Bop* / *Hot House* / *Toccata For Trumpet And Orchestra* / *Oop-Pop-A-Da* (vKH, DG) / *Things To Come* / *Yesterdays*

ELLA FITZGERALD (vocals); HANK JONES (piano) plus Dizzy Gillespie Orchestra:

Almost Like Being In Love (vEF) / *Stairway To The Stars* (vEF) / *Lover Man* (vEF) / *Flyin' Home* (vEF) / *Lady Be Good* (vEF) / *How High The Moon* (vEF)

Below: Dizzy Gillespie Orchestra with Ella Fitzgerald on stage at Carnegie Hall.

Dizzy, Bird, Ella Pack Carnegie

Despite Bad Acoustics, Gillespie Concert Offers Some Excellent Music

By MICHAEL LEVIN

New York—A sell-out crowd in huge Carnegie Hall heard the Dizzy Gillespie band aided by Charlie Parker plus vocal star Ella Fitzgerald run through 120 minutes of largely excellent music. Stand outs of the concert were George Russell's Cubano Bop, directed by the writer, John Lewis' Toccata For Trumpet, and Parker's altoing with the Quintet on numbers he and Gillespie recorded several years ago for Guild.

Miss Fitzgerald, on for the last part of the concert, showed to advantage in a white tailored dinner gown, running through a superb *Stairway To The Stars* and giving Dizzy considerable competition on some chase choruses of *How High The Moon*.

Principal fault of the concert was the acoustic balance. Promoter and commentator Leonard Feather who split the profits with Gillespie could have profited from the Granz concert in the same hall 18 hours earlier.

Granz placed the band mid-stage, and did not use the Carnegie Hall public address system with its speakers placed at the top of the arch. Instead, the band's vocalist and reedmen were heard through two speakers placed on each side of the stage.

Result of using the Hall speakers, placed at the acoustical peak point, was to give the same old barrel effect which has troubled other jazz concerts in the past.

Many Effects Lost

During many parts of the concert the reed section could not be heard while reed soloists, piano and vibraharp were usually among the missing.

Despite deficiencies of technique and intonation, which were marked in the Gillespie band, there is no getting around the fact that this is a unit which plays with profound conviction and enthusiasm.

Its ensemble playing has the same drive and communicative spirit that the old Basie and Goodman bands had in their hey-days. Evidently jazz bands like everything else have one period in their lives when they are thoroughly convinced that what they are playing is musically worthwhile and important and are able to convince their audiences of the same thing.

Stimulating Concert

No listener to the Gillespie concert, could miss the fact that unlike many other similar performances, here were musicians playing in a fashion they thought was best, not just a re-hash of other people's ideas.

By and large, the concert musically was stimulating. Dizzy was not at his best, clinkering and faltering occasionally. Each time he plays *Things To Come*, he insists on playing it faster, a shade difficult for even his iridescent technique to handle with ease and flow.

In the quintet numbers with Parker, Gillespie was appreciably bested. Parker's constant flow of ideas, his dramatic entrances and his perky use of musical punctuation was a revelation to an audience too often satiated by tenors.

Powerful, But Rough

The Gillespie band itself played with power, albeit roughly. Soloists sounded only good, largely because of the acoustic difficulties. John Lewis' piano, Milt Jackson's vibes and Cecil Payne's baritone were pretty well buried. Howard Johnson's tasty altoing of Tadd Dameron's *Nearness* came over as did Joe Harris' bootful drumming on *Salt Peanuts*.

The crowd unquestionably liked the *Cubano Bop* number with its added bongo and congo drum soloists the best, illustrating a point the *Beat* has often made: that there is much jazz can pick up on from the South American and Afro-Cuban rhythm styles.

Formalistically, the *Toccata* appealed to me: Lewis displayed an economy of means and an interesting series of ideas that make him a man to be watched in the writing field. Only fault with the score was its slightly pretentious ending a la Del Staigers of Goldman band fame.

New Bass Player

Al McKibbon, ex-Heard bass player, replaced Ray Brown who has left the band. McKibbon, as always played with a good beat and a big tone, but his lack of technical speed vice Brown made *One Bass Hit* less the showcase that it usually is.

There was a notable lack of shifting dynamics. Too often the Gillespie band plays loud or does not play. Period. The style espoused by this band is passing its birth pangs. It's time they stopped reaching and settled down to a little consistently good musicianship as well as unusual ideas.

One thing throughout the concert was completely inexcusable. Dizzy demands consideration from musicians and writers as a serious leader of a good musical band. No one, not even in Carnegie Hall, would want him to work without the showmanship so necessary to appeal to large crowds.

But this doesn't mean that he has the license to stand on a platform doing bumps, grinds and in general often acting like a darn fool.

Nor does it mean that while Ella Fitzgerald was singing that he should stand with a bouquet of flowers meant for her, doing mincing dance steps and in general stealing as much of the play from her singing as possible. This applies equally to the "nance-bow" taken by fine performer Babs Gonzales when called onstage for applause on his *Oopapada* score.

Gillespie is too fine a musician to have to indulge in shoddy tricks like this to garner attention. Showmanship is one thing. Acting like a bawdy house doorman is another.

In any concert of this sort, jazz musicians are on trial. There has been too much comment in the newspapers and press generally about the irresponsibility of the younger musicians for one of their leading lights to act like a bop buffoon instead of a boff performer.

SIDELIGHTS: Joe Harris played his drum solo with an old pair of shoes on, carefully parking his new brown kicks under the hi-hat cymbal stand… Dizzy changed suits during the intermission, caused much comment with display of a new and violent tie… The concert grossed over $5,300. With Ella Fitzgerald getting $500, Hall expenses and musicians, Feather and Gillespie still split around $2,000.

Thursday 9 October 1947

Dizzy Gillespie Orchestra open a one-week engagement at the Adams Theatre in Newark, New Jersey. Sharing top billing is Ella Fitzgerald.

Wednesday 15 October 1947

Dizzy Gillespie Orchestra close at the Adams Theatre in Newark, New Jersey.

Friday 17 October 1947

Dizzy Gillespie Orchestra play a concert in Binghamton, New York.

Saturday 18 October 1947

Dizzy Gillespie Orchestra play a concert at Cornell University. DIZZY GILLESPIE, DAVE BURNS, MATTHEW MCKAY, RAY ORR, ELMON WRIGHT (trumpets); TED KELLY, BILL SHEPHERD (trombones); JOHN BROWN, HOWARD JOHNSON (alto sax); JAMES MOODY, JOE GAYLES (tenor sax); CECIL PAYNE (baritone sax); JOHN LEWIS (piano); MILT JACKSON (vibes); AL MCKIBBON (bass); JOE HARRIS (drums); CHANO POZO (congas); KENNY HAGOOD (vocal)
Cool Breeze / I Can't Get Started / Relaxin' At Camarillo / Yesterdays / One Bass Hit / Salt Peanuts (vDG) / Night In Tunisia / Time After Time (vKH) / Groovin' High / Anthropology / Things To Come / You Go To My Head / Hot House / Lover Man / Toccata For Trumpet And Orchestra / The Nearness Of You / Mamselle / Oop-Pop-A-Da (vKH, DG) / Afro Cuban Drum Suite / You Go To My Head

Sunday 19 October 1947

Dizzy Gillespie Orchestra play a concert at Symphony Hall in Boston.

Tuesday 21 October 1947

Dizzy Gillespie's 30th birthday.

Wednesday 22 October 1947

Down Beat reviews Dizzy's latest Victor release:

Dizzy Gillespie
**** *Oopapada*
*** *OW*

Best recording the band has ever had in point of view of being in tune and balanced. Recording director Russ Case must have really sweated for the results. *Oopapada* is the tongue-in-cheek vocal riff duet worked out by Babs Gonzales. Diz and Kenny Hagood take turns singing unison and chase choruses, after the band amazingly enough kicks off the intro in clean fashion. Skipping the use of the trick vowel sounds for a moment, they get off some good vocal ideas. Dizzy's solo passage starts off with too much technique, ends with better ideas. Back of the sax solo the band's power, raw and unvarnished, comes through in searing quantities.

Unless the ear is way off, Ray Brown is playing bass on this date, and his tone on *Ow* is a sample of what is wrong with amplified basses at present when used with the gain too high and too much bass compensation. There are points when his notes sound like a tuba coming through cheese for clarity.

Gillespie's solo includes two fantastically long and well-expressed ideas. Other sections are not so well put together but these two passages are answers themselves to the people who feel that Gillespie never plays an integrated solo. (*Victor 20-2480*)

Friday 31 October 1947

Dizzy Gillespie Orchestra open a one-week engagement at the Apollo Theatre in New York City. Sharing top billing is Sarah Vaughan and also on the bill are the Two Zephyrs and Apus & Estrellita.

Thursday 6 November 1947

Dizzy Gillespie Orchestra close at the Apollo Theatre in New York City.

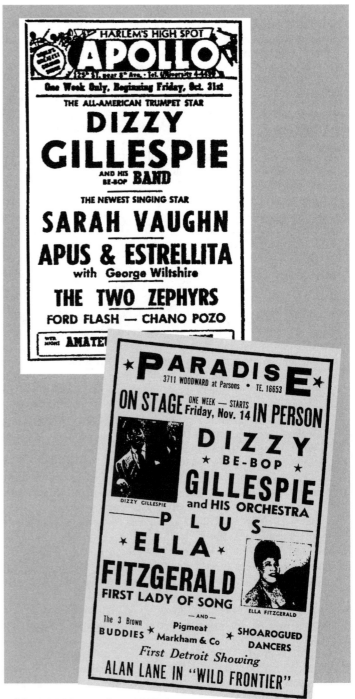

Friday 14 November 1947

Dizzy Gillespie Orchestra open at the Paradise Theatre, Detroit for a one-week engagement. Sharing top billing is Ella Fitzgerald.

Thursday 20 November 1947

Dizzy Gillespie Orchestra close at the Paradise Theatre, Detroit.

Friday 21 November 1947

Dizzy Gillespie Orchestra open at the El Sino in Detroit for a two-week engagement.

Thursday 4 December 1947

Dizzy Gillespie Orchestra close at the El Sino in Detroit.

Below: The Dizzy Gillespie Orchestra at the El Sino in Detroit.

Friday 5 December 1947

Dizzy Gillespie Orchestra open a one-week engagement at the Regal Theatre in Chicago. Sharing top billing is Nellie Lutcher.

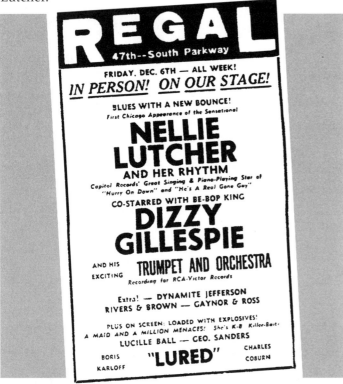

Thursday 11 December 1947

Dizzy Gillespie Orchestra close at the Regal Theatre, Chicago.

Saturday 13 December 1947

Dizzy Gillespie Orchestra play a one-nighter at the Club Riveria in St. Louis.

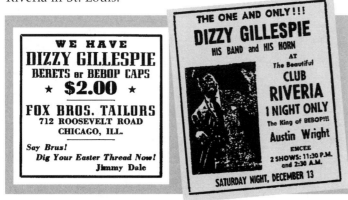

Sunday 21 December 1947

Dizzy Gillespie records with the Metronome All-Stars for Columbia in New York City.

DIZZY GILLESPIE (trumpet); BILL HARRIS (trombone); BUDDY DE FRANCO (clarinet); FLIP PHILLIPS (tenor sax); NAT KING COLE (piano); BILLY BAUER (guitar); EDDIE SAFRANSKI (bass); BUDDY RICH (drums)

Leap Here

At the same session the Stan Kenton Orchestra record *Metronome Riff* as the Metronome All-Stars.

Monday 22 December 1947

Dizzy Gillespie Orchestra record for Victor in New York City.

DIZZY GILLESPIE, DAVE BURNS, LAMAR WRIGHT JR, BENNY BAILEY, ELMON WRIGHT (trumpets); TED KELLY, BILL SHEPHERD (trombones); JOHN BROWN, HOWARD JOHNSON (alto sax); GEORGE NICHOLAS, JOE GAYLES (tenor sax); CECIL PAYNE (baritone sax); JOHN LEWIS (piano); AL McKIBBON (bass); KENNY CLARKE (drums); CHANO POZO (conga); KENNY HAGOOD (vocal)

Algo Bueno / Cool Breeze (vDG, KH) / *Cubana Be / Cubana Bop*

Friday 26 December 1947

Dizzy Gillespie Orchestra appear in concert with Sarah Vaughan at the Brooklyn Academy of Music in Brooklyn, New York City.

Saturday 27 December 1947

Dizzy Gillespie Orchestra appear in a Fred Robbins One Nite Stand concert at Town Hall in New York City. Timmie Rogers is also on the bill.

Tuesday 30 December 1947

Dizzy Gillespie Orchestra record for Victor in New York City.

DIZZY GILLESPIE, DAVE BURNS, LAMAR WRIGHT JR, BENNY BAILEY, ELMON WRIGHT (trumpets); TED KELLY, BILL SHEPHERD (trombones); JOHN BROWN, HOWARD JOHNSON (alto sax); GEORGE NICHOLAS, JOE GAYLES (tenor sax); CECIL PAYNE (baritone sax); JOHN LEWIS (piano); AL McKIBBON (bass); KENNY CLARKE (drums); CHANO POZO (conga); KENNY HAGOOD (vocal)

Manteca / Good Bait / Ool-Ya-Koo (vDG, KH) / *Minor Walk / Woody'n'You*

1948

Wednesday 7 January 1948

Dizzy Gillespie Orchestra appear in concert at Carnegie Hall in New York City.

Diz To Bop Swedes First

New York—Dizzy Gillespie opens his European tour January 26 at Gothenburg, Sweden.

Diz Sails For Europe

New York—Paced by a massed salute from the Stan Kenton band at the pier, the Dizzy Gillespie band set sail for Europe January 16 aboard the steamer Drottingholm for a continental tour including Scandanavia, the lowlands, Switzerland and England. The Kenton band, whose leader is known to be highly anxious to make a European trip, arrived at the pier at 10:30 a. m. to serenade the Gillespie band as it boarded ship, then raced back to the Paramount to play a twelve o'clock show.

Gillespie's itinerary includes: January 26, Gothenburg, Sweden; January 28, Stockholm; 29, Orebro; 30, Borlange; 31, Vasteras; February 1, Storvik; 2, Stockholm; 3, Norkoeping; 4, Malmo; (all of the preceeding in Sweden). February 6, the band plays a concert in Prague, Czechoslovakia, moves on to Copenhagen, then perhaps an occupied zone date in Germany; February 11 in Amsterdam, Holland; 12, in Brussels, Belgium; 14 in Paris, two weeks from February 16 in Switzerland, two dates in England, March 2 and 4, with a return to the states slated for March 5.

Another Jazz Tome!

New York—Before sailing for Europe, Dizzy Gillespie made a writing deal with Leonard Feather, swing critic, magazine and radio writer, for a book on modern jazz. The two will collaborate, Feather doing research and outline work during Gillespie's overseas junket. Publication rights, while not yet sold, probably will go to J. J. Robbins.

British Waived Rules To 'Catch Gillespie'

London—A spokesman for the British musicians' union is said to have revealed that the waiving of rules which might have prevented Dizzy Gillespie's local engagements, was prompted by three considerations.

First, Gillespie's band, according to popular consensus, is the outstanding exponent of the new be-bop style of music; secondly, any proposed booking would be for a short time rather than for an extended tour and, therefore, would not replace British musicians, and, lastly, the music profession itself is anxious to hear this outstanding exhibitor of a brand new music, of which he is the acknowledged creator.

Bands Across The Sea

While the immediate decision benefits Gillespie it can readily be seen that the heretofore stringent restrictive attitude of local musicians has been somewhat relaxed and, therefore, opens the door to exchanges of musical aggregations between English musicians and those of other countries. Such exchanges would, naturally, be mutual.

One of the interesting sidelights on this special consideration for Dizzy Gillespie is the report that the union's decision was based upon a petition drawn up by musicians themselves, begging the board to relax its ban so that they might see the exponent of be-bop.

Friday 16 January 1948

Dizzy Gillespie Orchestra leave New York City bound for Sweden.

Below: Dizzy poses aboard the Drottningholm with manager Milt Shaw and Leonard Feather just before the band sails for Sweden.

Monday 26 January 1948

The Drottningholm is late arriving in Gothenburg where the orchestra is due to play an 8 o'clock concert at the Mässhallen. The weary Dizzy Gillespie Orchestra eventually arrive at the theatre at 10 o'clock and play their first concert in Sweden to a half-empty hall.

Tuesday 27 January 1948

Dizzy Gillespie Orchestra play three concerts at the Vinterpalatset in Stockholm, Sweden. Swedish jazz authority Rolf Dahlgren remembers:

> THE THREE CONCERTS WERE ARRANGED IN A BIG DANCE HALL (CAPACITY c.1400). I HEARD THEM ALL. THE FIRST CONCERT HAD SOLD MAYBE A HALF HOUSE – PERHAPS 700. THE SECOND A LITTLE LESS, SAY 400–500. BEFORE THAT CONCERT ENDED ONE OF THE POOR PROMOTERS WENT ON STAGE AND BEGGED THOSE PRESENT TO STAY OVER BECAUSE THERE WERE ONLY 200 TICKETS SOLD.

Wednesday 28 January 1948

Dizzy Gillespie Orchestra play a concert in Karlstad, Sweden.

Thursday 29 January 1948

Dizzy Gillespie Orchestra play a concert in Örebro, Sweden.

Friday 30 January 1948

Dizzy Gillespie Orchestra play in Borlange, Sweden.

Saturday 31 January 1948

Dizzy Gillespie Orchestra play in Västerås, Sweden.

Sunday 1 February 1948

Dizzy Gillespie Orchestra play a concert in Gåvle followed by another in Storvik, Sweden.

Dizzyites, Mal De Mer Make Eventful Crossing

Stockholm—Mother Sills and the boys in Dizzy Gillespie's band became almost constant companions on the trip here from the States, it was learned when the S.S. Drottningholm landed with them. Mr. Be-Bop himself encountered trouble on the first day of sailing. Meeting unusually heavy weather, the ship tossed constantly with the result that the leader became dizzy (no pun intended) and suffered a minor head injury when he fell to the deck. This convinced him that his bunk was a much safer place and 'twas there he spent the remainder of the trip.

As the tardy ship neared Gothenberg, it was learned the band would not be landed until long after the initial concert was slated to start. Through the influence of the captain of the Drottningholm, manager Milt Shaw commandeered one of three tugs standing by the ship and brought his seasick musicians ashore on that, getting them onto the bandstand a full two hours after scheduled starting time. Despite this, 14,000 persons attended.

Swedes Mob Halls To Dig The Dizzy

STOCKHOLM—America's latest jazz phenomenon—be-bop music—has taken this jazz music hotbed by storm during the last few weeks as devotees of popular music packed every nook and cranny of the Vinterpalaset to hear the dispensations of Dizzy Gillespie, great American trumpeter.

Every attendance record ever established has been broken to smithereens as the goateed American and his amazing aggregation have played to capacity crowds on three different occasions.

Originally the band was to play a single concert but there were so many patrons unable to gain admission that an encore was arranged only to have the same situation develop, thus necessitating a third date. Once again there was a sellout enabling the Diz to set a record of 26,749 paid admissions for the three concerts.

Monday 2 February 1948
Dizzy Gillespie Orchestra play two concerts at the Vinterpalatset in Stockholm, Sweden. Part of the performance is recorded.
DIZZY GILLESPIE, DAVE BURNS, LAMAR WRIGHT JR, BENNY BAILEY, ELMON WRIGHT (trumpets); TED KELLY, BILL SHEPHERD (trombones); JOHN BROWN, HOWARD JOHNSON (alto sax); GEORGE NICHOLAS, JOE GAYLES (tenor sax); CECIL PAYNE (baritone sax); JOHN LEWIS (piano); AL McKIBBON (bass); KENNY CLARKE (drums); CHANO POZO (conga); KENNY HAGOOD (vocal); FOLKE OLHAGEN (announcer)
I Waited For You (theme) / *Our Delight* / *I Can't Get Started* / *Ool-Ya-Koo* (vDG, KH) / *Manteca* / *More Than You Know* / *Mamselle* (vKH) / *Oo-Pop-A-Da* (vDG, KH) / *Ray's Idea* / *I Waited For You* (theme)

Tuesday 3 February 1948
Dizzy Gillespie Orchestra play in Norrköping, Sweden.

Wednesday 4 February 1948
Dizzy Gillespie Orchestra play a concert in Malmö, Sweden.

Thursday 5 February 1948
Dizzy Gillespie Orchestra play a concert in Helsingborg, Sweden.

Friday 6 February 1948
Dizzy Gillespie Orchestra play a concert in Gothenburg, Sweden.

Saturday 7 February 1948
Dizzy Gillespie Orchestra play a concert in Varberg, Sweden.

Sunday 8 February 1948
Dizzy Gillespie Orchestra play a concert in Halmstad, Sweden. Concerts in Czechoslovakia, Holland and Germany are cancelled, as is a proposed two-week stay in Switxerland.

Wednesday 11 February 1948
Dizzy Gillespie Orchestra play a concert in Antwerp, Belgium. The concert is promoted by the Hot Club and emceed by Carlos De Radzitzky.

Down Beat reviews Dizzy's latest Victor release:

Dizzy Gillespie
*** *TwoBass Hit*
*** *Stay On It*
   Al McKibbon plays bass on this follow-up to the Ray Brown bass specialty, *One Bass Hit*. Dizzy's solo starts out more restrainedly and with better tone than usual. The bass pick-up during band passages is not as clear as it should be, making it hard to hear McKibbon's ideas. On neither of these sides does the band sound as impressive as it did on its first Victor sides. Sloppy execution is one fault, the band's constant lack of solo strength another. (*Victor 20-2603*)

Thursday 12 February 1948
Dizzy Gillespie Orchestra play a concert in Brussels, Belgium. The concert is emceed by Carlos De Radzitzky.

Saturday 14 February 1948
Dizzy Gillespie Orchestra play a concert at the Apollo Theatre in Paris, France.

Friday 20 February 1948
Dizzy Gillespie Orchestra play a concert (8.45pm) at the Salle Pleyel in Paris, France.

Sunday 22 February 1948
Dizzy Gillespie Orchestra play a matinee concert (2.30pm) at the Salle Pleyel in Paris, France.

Monday 28 February 1948
Dizzy Gillespie Orchestra play a concert at the Salle Pleyel in Paris. The concert is recorded.
DIZZY GILLESPIE, DAVE BURNS, LAMAR WRIGHT JR, BENNY BAILEY, ELMON WRIGHT (trumpets); TED KELLY, BILL SHEPHERD (trombones); JOHN BROWN, HOWARD JOHNSON (alto sax); GEORGE NICHOLAS, JOE GAYLES (tenor sax); CECIL PAYNE (baritone sax); JOHN LEWIS (piano); AL McKIBBON (bass); KENNY CLARKE (drums); CHANO POZO (conga); KENNY HAGOOD (vocal)
'Round Midnight / *Algo Bueno* / *I Can't Get Started* / *Ool-Ya-Koo* (vDG, KH) / *Afro-Cubano Suite* / *Things To Come* / *Oop-Pop-A-Da* (vDG, KH) / *Two Bass Hit* / *Good Bait*

Wednesday 3 March 1948
Dizzy Gillespie Orchestra play a concert (8.30–10.30pm) at the Palais d'Hiver in Lyons, France.

Friday 5 March 1948
Dizzy Gillespie Orchestra play a 'Grand Gala de la Presse' concert in Marseilles, France. The Peters Sisters and Mezz Mezzrow are also featured.

Friday 12 March 1948
The Dizzy Gillespie Orchestra board the SS DeGrasse for the trip home to New York. Drummer Kenny Clarke opts to stay in France and Dizzy, manager Milt Shaw and bongoist Chano Pozo prefer to fly.

Thursday 18 March 1948
The Dizzy Gillespie Orchestra arrive in New York.

Friday 5 March 1948
Dizzy Gillespie Orchestra play a hastily arranged welcome home concert at Town hall in New York City.

Stories on Dizzy Gillespie flooded the news desks around here before the outfit had even set sail for the States. Financial embarrassments, jails, lack of travel facilities, all were heavily publicized.

Diz Disappointed

Much of this was explained by Billy Shaw, partner of booker Moe Gale and personal manager of Dizzy, who flew over and back to straighten out the complications. According to Billy, the advance guarantee in American money was not posted here before the band set sail for Sweden. The deal with the European called for $5,500 per week, the band to get $2,000 over there, the balance to be posted in this country in American money. Restrictions on taking money out of European countries necessitated such an arrangement. This is customary among American units playing overseas these days.

Not only wasn't the money posted but, Billy claims, the band was not paid off in full after it played its engagements over there. In fact, he claims, half the money still is forthcoming. Of course, such incidents happen on dates with the best of bands and promoters with "the best intentions" right here in this country, so it is not a practice peculiar to Europe.

Billy jailed

Billy explained the jail incident, which occurred in Sweden, as the outcome of an argument between one of the promoting partners ("the bad one") and himself. The other partner ("the good one") didn't enter into this. It seems the promoter ("the bad one") hemmed and hawed about paying and, when Billy showed up with an attorney, cast some verbal reflections on the Shaw religious heritage. A nearby metal candlestick found its way into Billy's hand and, in turn, to the promoter's skull. The

promoter must have been a hard headed soul, for Billy didn't spend much time in the Swedish hoosegow.

When it came time to depart for the States, Shaw explained that the home office sent money for the band to return third class on the S.S. America. Billy could have got better accommodations on the French liner De Grasse, thus the argument with the home office on transportation. The band did come back on the De grasse, aided by money from the home office, necessary, Shaw explained, because the promoters had not paid off "in full."

Dizzy hopes to return to again play the Scandinavian countries, France, etc., but, his manager hastens to add, for different promoters this trip.

Milt Shaw, Dizzy's band manager and son of Billy, merely commented, "Never again."

europe goes dizzy
mad management can't stop glad hand extended to bop in sweden, denmark, belgium, and france

by leonard feather

DIZZY IS BACK, but the melody, and Kenny Clarke, lingered on. Minus a drummer who had decided to stay in France for keeps, the Gillespie group returned to these shores on March 18, preceded on a plane by Diz himself, manager Milt Shaw and bongoist Chano Pozo, who had said he couldn't face another ship trip and insisted on flying.

Just two months had elapsed since the band had sailed from New York. Into those months were crowded a wild variety of episodes, starting with a sorry chapter of multiple seasickness and proceeding through many managerial mishaps to a happy ending.

"We started out on the wrong foot," recalls Diz. "We were set for a concert in Gothenburg, Sweden, at 8:30 the night of January 26, and our ship was due in the day before. By 10:15 on the 26th we were still a 20-minute boat ride from the shore at Gothenburg and they had to send a tugboat out to pick us up. Plenty of people had waited, though, and we started the concert—two and a half hours late."

That wasn't the end of the first night's troubles. Some of the band (including Milt Shaw) couldn't find accommodations and had to walk the streets all night. On a subsequent return to Gothenburg they got to town at 4 AM and found no rooms, and paced the pavements until noon.

This was just the beginning of the difficulties, however. Harold Lundquist, who had promoted the trip and guaranteed to have half the money deposited in a American bank before the band left this country, had reneged on this promise, and even after Dizzy's arrival in Sweden continued to stall on payments. This continued while the band played a series of dates in Sweden. Musically, everything was fine. "The Swedes really liked the music," recalls Dizzy, "and Denmark was the greatest—we played to nine thousand people in one afternoon and evening, doing three concerts all the same day."

Another thing that amazed Dizzy was the type of audiences they played for—"Not just the young crowd we'd get in the States, but people from six to sixty! We even saw old men with crutches applauding and hollering. The crowds wouldn't stop until I put up my hand to announce the next tune, and then they'd be so quiet you could hear a pin drop."

Next, the band headed for Belgium, where the Hot Clubs were promoting Diz in cooperation with Lundquist. Things now came to a head; Milt had exchanged several calls with his father in New York (Billy Shaw, the band's booker) and it was decided that the band would refuse to work until all money due them was paid up. Billy decided to fly to Sweden to straighten out the mixup.

The bewildered Belgians, caught in the middle of this, had to arrange to give Milt Shaw enough money to provide a week's salary for the band; meanwhile Charles Delaunay, who had called Dizzy from Paris, sent an emissary to Brussels to take over from Lundquist the responsibility for the rest of the European trip.

Around this time the band was, according to its original schedule, due to play in Amsterdam and Prague followed by a full week in Switzerland, but Lundquist had been changing the route almost daily and these dates were called off. The British Ministry of Labor's decision, overriding the permission granted by the English Musicians' Union to let the band play some concerts in London, was another blow.

Anyway, Brussels was great, and the audience enthusiasm had compensated in part for the booking troubles, though the men in the band at this point were about ready to kill Lundquist. By the time Billy Shaw got to see Lundquist in Sweden, the band was in Paris. There were some bitter exchanges between Shaw and Lundquist, at the climax of which the latter called Billy "a dirty lying Jew."

Provoked beyond endurance, the mercurial Billy seized a table lamp and bopped the delinquent promoter, with the result that both of them were incarcerated (Billy only for a couple of hours). Lundquist, who turned out to have been forging the names of his alleged backers and misusing funds that didn't belong to him, was indicted on a variety of charges and was still in jail when Billy left to join the band in Paris.

Paris was more than ready for Dizzy. The eager Delaunay, ready to show that Panassié's alleged Jazz Festival in Nice was hardly representative of current trends in jazz, sold out three Gillespie concerts at the Salle Pleyel and had the band doubling at the Champs Elysées Club and later at the Ambassadeurs.

"Paris was a little different from Scandinavia—the audiences, I mean," says Diz. "A younger, wilder crowd. And of course I hardly knew the place, it had changed so much. I met very few people who'd known me when I was there with Teddy Hill's band—after all, that was almost eleven years ago."

During its stay in Paris the band, which had been living in the same or adjacent hotels every night, spread out all over town and began to find time for a little fun and entertainment of its own. Dizzy had done plenty of shopping in Scandinavia, his purchases including a Leica camera, a meerschaum pipe, and a Russian cossack hat which he wore throughout the tour.

The band played one theatre date in Paris— oddly enough, the theatre a namesake of Harlem's own Apollo. From Paris, the boppers proceeded to Lyons and Marseilles, spending two days in each city and playing a concert in Marseilles at which the Mezz Mezzrow band and the peters Sisters were also featured. The Moldy Fig music of the Mezzrow men was a source of astonishment to Dizzy's musicians; no less surprising, says Dizzy, was the equally hearty applause accorded to both orchestras.

Returning to Paris and playing a couple more days at the Ambassadeurs, the band began to get homesick for wives and families, and with no further bookings set it only remained for adequate accommodation home to be provided. A booking on the Queen Mary from Southampton had been canceled by Lundquist and a large sum had to be wired by Billy Shaw to enable the band to buy its fares home. At the last moment they obtained passage on the De Grasse, embarking on what turned out to be a less nerve-wracking ordeal than the shaky eastbound trip on the Drottningholm two months earlier.

Friday 30 April 1948

Dizzy Gillespie Orchestra open a one-week engagement at the Apollo Theatre in New York City. Also on the bill are the Beale Street Boys, Rivers & Brown, Al Hylton and Billy Nightingale.

Thursday 6 May 1948

Dizzy Gillespie Orchestra close at the Apollo Theatre in New York City.

Saturday 8 May 1948

Dizzy Gillespie Orchestra play a midnight concert at Carnegie Hall in New York City. Woody Herman presents Dizzy with Varsity Magazine's 'Musician of the Year' award and the concert, promoted by Leonard Feather, premieres Dizzy's 'Swedish Suite'.

Dizzy Gillespie, playing a midnight bash following a Saturday concert, failed to live up to expectations, drawing a good $4,000 but still losing about $100 for promoter Leonard Feather. Previous appearances by Dizzy and his band at Town Hall, just after his arrival from Europe, and the Apollo theater for a week before the concert, probably can be blamed for the be-bopper's missing a sellout at Carnegie.

Above: Dizzy receives his Varsity Magazine award from Woody Herman.
Below: Backstage at Carnegie Hall, Dizzy premieres his 'Swedish Suite' for promoter Leonard Feather and Miss Sweden.

Diz Trains For Carnegie Date

New York—Dizzy Gillespie gave his band a general shakeup followed by a series of rehearsals in preparation for his Carnegie Hall concert, Saturday midnight, May 8.

Hampton Reese, French horn, was moved in on the recommendation of trumpeter Miles Davis. Two new saxes were brought in; Ernie Henry, alto, and Ray Abrams, tenor. Henry was on 52nd Street not too long ago playing with Tadd Dameron at the Onyx. He replaced Howard Johnson; Abrams took over for George Nicholas.

Brass Changes

Willie Cooper replaced Lammar Wright Jr., in the trumpet section, and Candy Ross, formerly heard with Mercer Ellington, was added on trombone, giving the band three.

The rhythm section also was overhauled with Teddy Stewart back on drums; Tadd Dameron on piano and Gracham Moncur on bass.

Replaced Kenny

At press time, Dizzy and his arranger, Walter Fuller, were auditioning girl singers to replace Kenny (Pancho) Hagood.

The Carnegie bash, incidentally, will be repeated the following Tuesday, May 11, at the Academy of Music in Philadelphia.

Tuesday 11 May 1948
Dizzy Gillespie Orchestra repeat the concert at the Academy of Music in Philadelphia.

Sunday 16 May 1948
Dizzy Gillespie Orchestra play a dance at the New Savoy Ballroom in Chicago.

Thursday 27 May 1948
Dizzy Gillespie Orchestra play a concert for Norman Granz at the Syria Mosque in Pittsburgh.

Thursday 10 June 1948
Dizzy Gillespie Orchestra open a three-night engagement at the Rajah Theatre in Reading, Pennsylvania.

Saturday 12 June 1948
Dizzy Gillespie Orchestra close at the Rajah Theatre in Reading, Pennsylvania.

Wednesday 16 June 1948
Dizzy Gillespie Orchestra open a two-week engagement at the Royal Roost in New York City opposite Thelonious Monk.

Down Beat reviews Dizzy's latest Victor release:

Dizzy Gillespie
** *Good Bait*
** *Ool-Ya-Koo*

Somehow big band bop doesn't ever quite seem to come off except when it's used as an accessory after the fact by bands like the old Herman Herd or Krupa's more dignified adaptations. Even when Dizzy is up front, it's ponderous, noisy and sloppy for the most part. There are points of interest on both sides here, for example in the high unison brass behind the alto chorus in Ool and the tail end of **Bait**, but all in all it's a muddy performance. **Ool** is 50 per cent pre-occupied with scatting gibberish by Diz and Ken Hagood, while **Bait** has some fair portions of his trumpet work. (**Victor 20-2878**)

Tuesday 29 June 1948
Dizzy Gillespie Orchestra close at the Royal Roost in New York City.

Wednesday 30 June 1948
Dizzy Gillespie Orchestra play a one-nighter in Asbury Park, New Jersey.

Thursday 1 July 1948
Dizzy Gillespie Orchestra play a one-nighter in Newark, New Jersey.

All-Stars to Roost

New York—Dizzy Gillespie wound up a smash two-week bop at Broadway's Royal Roost, being replaced by the International All-Stars, a group made up of Georgie Auld, tenor sax; Bill Harris, trombone; Chubby Jackson, bass; Shelly Manne, drums, and Lou Levy, piano.

Below: The building that housed the Royal Roost, pictured in 1990 shortly before being demolished to make way for a hotel. Pictured from the corner of Broadway and 48th Street.

Saturday 3 July 1948

Dizzy Gillespie Orchestra play a one-nighter in Philadelphia.

Sunday 4 July 1948

Dizzy Gillespie Orchestra play a one-nighter in Atlantic City, New Jersey. Dizzy hears Johnny Hartman singing in a club and offers him a job.

Monday 5 July 1948

Dizzy Gillespie Orchestra play a one-nighter in Buckroe Beach, Virginia before heading for the West Coast.

Friday 16 July 1948

Dizzy Gillespie Orchestra play a one-nighter at the Trianon Ballroom in San Francisco.

Saturday 17 July 1948

Dizzy Gillespie Orchestra play a concert at the Auditorium in Oakland. *Down Beat* reviewer, Ralph J. Gleason, is at both the Bay area performances:

Dizzy Gillespie To Appear At Pasadena Auditorium, July 19

HOLLYWOOD, Calif.—Gene Norman, local disc jockey who has successfully introduced the jazz concert medium to Southern California music fans, announced that the famous trumpet player, Dizzy Gillespie, is scheduled for his first local appearance in the Pasadena Civic Auditorium on Monday evening, July 19th.

Appearing with his new big band, Gillespie is probably one of the foremost figures in the jazz world today. Famous for his "bebop principles", Dizzy is widely noted for his tremendous contribution to contemporary music. Lovers of music throughout the world were quick to recognise the technique and interpretations of Dizzy's and have adopted him with frantic enthusiasm.

Gillespie, before organizing his own band, was associated with such musical greats as Lionel Hampton, Duke Ellington, Charlie Barnet, Benny Carter, Jimmy Dorsey and Artie Shaw. He has been featured on hundreds of recordings and finally had to form his own orchestra because of public demand. When New York's famous highway of jazz, 52nd street, heard him several years ago, Gillespie was immediately acknowledged as one of the all-time great trumpet virtuosi.

The promoter of the recent smash Hollywood Bowl jazz affairs, Gene Norman is proud to present the startling artistry of Dizzy Gillespie and his orchestra in their first California performance. Norman also announces that the talent lineup will include other stellar performers on July 19, in Pasadena.

Small Crowds Grow As Diz Bops Frisco

Reviewed at the Trianon ballroom, San Francisco.

John Brown, tenor; Ernest Henry, alto; James Moody, alto; Joe Gayles, tenor; Cecil Payne, baritone.
Dave Burns, William Cook, Elman Wright, trumpets.
William Shepherd, Jesse Tarrant, trombones.
Nelson Boyd, bass; James Forman, piano; Teddy Stewart, drums.
Luciana Pozo Gonzales (called Chano), conga drum.

San Francisco—Dizzy Gillespie bopped the Bay City for a one-niter at the Trianon ballroom out in Fillmore and blew up such a storm that by the time he left town he was all set for a two-week date beginning August 18 at Barney Deazy's O'Farrell street spot, Blanco's Cotton Club. However, the whole deal fell through because of "contractual difficulties," leaving Diz unbooked until he got the spot at Billy Berg's. A small crowd of Bay City boppers braved the door tab of $1,85 to catch Diz at the Trianon, but a larger contingent came out to greet him in Oakland the following night where he played to a crowd of 3,000 at the Oakland auditorium.

Reception to the band was mixed. The crowd was heavily filled both nights with musicians and almost without exception they were super-enthusiastic about the band and its music. Dancers were the most skeptical, although many of them seemed to get as big a kick out of Dizzy's group as the musicians did.

Heavy Sked

After leaving this area, Dizzy was set to open July 27 for three weeks at the Cricket Club in L. A., then shift over to Billy Berg's. Following that, they play the Regal theater in Chicago beginning September 17, then return to New York for two weeks at the Roost.

John Hartman, ex-Earl Hines vocalist was set to join the band in L. A., and Mathew Gee is slated to join the trombone section when the band returns to New York.

Assorted Fans

Dizzy drew a varied assortment of customers in his two dates here. Mixed in with musicians and general public were a lot of customers who were there purely to see what it was the band does that causes so much excitement. Dizzy did his best to oblige them, knocking off

number after number with the peculiar precision and force that characterizes this band.

On both ballads like *Don't Blame Me* and *Someone to Watch Over Me*, and Gillespie specials such as *Manteca, Second Balcony Jump, Good Bait, Emanon, Things to Come* and others, the band played superbly both nights from start to finish. By the time Dizzy got through playing *Manteca* and seated himself on top of the piano to play *Second Balcony Jump* the crowd was absolutely wild.

The audience, both nights, although naturally less familiar with the band than New York audiences, still showed that the arguments of Dizzy's critics—that his music is without form—are worthless.Many members of the audience had memorized the arrangements and sang them along with the band—which couldn't be done if there weren't some definite pattern. Otherwise, you might beep when you should bop, and that would never do.

"It's the Thing"

"Listen," a Local 6 man said during one of the intermissions, "you can't get away from the fact that that stuff is the thing now. Everywhere you go you hear a little bop even on the radio, and any musician who misses hearing this band doesn't deserve to be a musician." Well, that's putting it rather strong, but as an ex-moldy fig, we can say it's the experience not to be duplicated. This observer can only think of two other bands which generate such excitement—Ellington and Hampton—and that's as strong as we know how to put it.

Dizzy is without question the star of his own band. However, every man in it, known or unknown, seems to be star in his own right. John Brown and Joe Gayles blow a lot of tenor, and Ernie Henry is excellent on alto. The trumpet section is a joy to hear—precise, smooth, well-drilled, and capable of fine work even without Dizzy to spur them on. Stars of the band, aside from Diz, to this writer, are Teddy Stewart, who lays down a terrific beat and performs wonderfully throughout all the intricate arrangements the band specializes in, and Chano, the conga drummer, who for sheer exuberance, is hard to beat.

He and Stewart have so many rhythmic patterns worked out between them that they seem almost to act as one man many times. All in all, this is a Class A band even if you don't like bop. And if you do like it, it's the band to beat all bands.

Monday 19 July 1948

Dizzy Gillespie Orchestra play a concert at the Pasadena Civic Auditorium in Pasadena, Los Angeles. Vocalist Johnny Hartman maes his debut with the band.

DIZZY GILLESPIE, DAVE BURNS, WILLIE COOK, ELMON WRIGHT (trumpets); JESSE TARRANT, BILL SHEPHERD (trombones); JOHN BROWN, ERNIE HENRY (alto sax); JAMES MOODY, JOE GAYLES (tenor sax); CECIL PAYNE (baritone sax); JAMES FOREMAN JR (piano); NELSON BOYD (bass); TEDDY STEWART (drums); CHANO POZO (conga)

Emanon / One Bass Hit / Good Bait / Manteca / Ool-Ya-Koo (vDG, JB) / Stay On It / 'Round About Midnight / Algo Bueno / I Can't Get Started / Groovin' High / Cubana Be, Cubana Bop

Tuesday 20 July 1948

Dizzy Gillespie Orchestra open a one-week engagement at the Million Dollar Theatre in Los Angeles.

Monday 26 July 1948

Dizzy Gillespie Orchestra close at the Million Dollar Theatre in Los Angeles.

Dizzy Parodists Travel Along

Hollywood—The flowering of bop, on Dizzy's tie at least, seems to interest writer Ollie Britton, left, and comedians Melvin White and Willie Lewis, who flank the Diz. Britton wrote a take-off on bop for Lewis and White which so impressed Gillespie that he has the team traveling with him. They were signed for four weeks at the Cricket club here following their date at the Million Dollar theater.

Wednesday 28 July 1948

Dizzy Gillespie Orchestra open a three-week engagement at the Cricket Club in Los Angeles.

Tuesday 17 August 1948

Dizzy Gillespie Orchestra close at the Cricket Club in Los Angeles.

Wednesday 18 August 1948

Dizzy Gillespie Orchestra play a dance in Los Angeles.

Thursday 19 August 1948

Dizzy Gillespie Orchestra open a three-week engagement at Billy Berg's in Los Angeles.

Gillespie Settles Down in Hollywood at Berg's

HOLLYWOOD, Calif.—Following his opening Thursday night, Dizzy Gillespie settled down for a three weeks run at Billy Berg's nightery here, marking the first appearance of the bebop king's orchestra at the spot.

Wednesday 8 September 1948

Dizzy Gillespie Orchestra close at Billy Berg's in Los Angeles. Dizzy and the Orchestra play a one-nighter at Edgewater Beach in San Francisco before going on to one-nighters in Denver, Omaha and Milwaukee en route to Chicago.

Even Dixiecats Turn Out For Gillespie's One-Niter

By RALPH J. GLEASON

San Francisco—Dizzy Gillespie's one-niter at the Edgewater Beach here came on like a bass drum bop at the end of two weeks of Lionel Hampton's music, giving the town a climax to the best stretch of big band music it's had in a long time. Gillespie, sounding much more settled down than when he played here on his way to L.A. in July, brought a crowd of 1,200 out to the Beach to outdraw such bands as Woody Herman, Stan Kenton, and Duke Ellington.

Big boot for local boppers in Diz's band was the presence of Andy Duryea, local trombonist who joined Diz when he was here this summer. Duryea, ignored by many local musicians this past year, has blossomed forth as one of the stars of the Gillespie mob and is a featured soloist on trombone and bass trumpet.

Crowd with Diz

James Moody, tenorman wrongly credited in our review here in August 25 issue as an altoman, grabbed plenty of raves locally for his work. Crowd was completely with Diz this time, and the enthusiasm generated was potent enough to bust the atom.

Even local Dixieland musicians turned out for Diz … one of them took the night off at a cost of 15 iron men which is about as deep a compliment as you can pay.

Another heavy compliment for Diz came from Lester Bass, Hampton trombonist, who said it was the best big band Dizzy has ever had and added that he should know, having worked in one of them himself.

At any rate it was one of the most sensational evenings San Francisco music circles have had in some time. Dizzy came in for plenty of praise locally as a leader, too.

Slates One-Niters

Band left for one-niters in Denver and Omaha and a week in Milwaukee before returning to New York. Diz is booked for a return to Billy Berg's next January and possibly a date here at the Cotton Club.

Diz Presents Milwaukee A 'Clean' Band

Milwaukee—A well-rehearsed Dizzy Gillespie band that presented clean-cut arrangements and never sounded stiff or overarranged received a well-deserved hand at its concert here.

The band fortified its soloists with striking, subdued backgrounds which showed each man working with, rather than fighting, the guy sitting next to him.

Arranging Helps

Don't Blame Me, an outstanding number, benefited especially from Walter Fuller's fine arranging plus Gillespie's delicate phrasing. A light-fingered, fluent piano by Jimmy Forman didn't hurt the piece either.

Vocalist Johnny Hartman did acceptably well with *They Say It's Wonderful* and *I Should Care*, but both would sound better if he had enunciated more clearly. Diz plugged a couple of his records with *Manteca* and *Things To Come* which were even more up tempo than the recordings.

Manteca, written by Diz and Chano Pozo, the bongo drummer, was done almost as a tribal rite, becoming downright primitive.

Friday 17 September 1948

Dizzy Gillespie Orchestra open a one-week engagement at the Regal Theatre in Chicago.

Wednesday 22 September 1948

Down Beat reviews Dizzy's latest Victor release:

Dizzy Gillespie
**** *Manteca*
*** *Cool Breeze*

Unfortunately I've never heard the mighty Diz in the flesh though from what I've read and heard on wax of his big band the quality thereof seems to depend on the time of day, who happens to be playing in the band, how many rehearsals there were, and a few other variables. What develops as a result of these factors can be either very good or mediocre.

Well, anyhow, when they cut these two the signs of the zodiac must have been in complete agreement because they are an elegant coupling, showing off both Diz and his big band to the best possible advantage. Both are completely instrumental save for a bop vocal on the A side. This *Manteca* is the one that breas up the show while Diz is doing theaters, and the report is understandable because it's a thrilling arrangement and spots some fluent Diz.

Both use the Afro-Cuban rhythmic pattern that he has done so much with of late, and the combination of this type of beat and bop figures and orchestration is dynamite. *Manteca* has a rhythm section opener and builds one section on another gradually until Diz enters in a splash of technique, after which the rhythm has it alone for a few bars before the ensemble which works brass against saxes and vice versa.

The band figures in support of the tenor chorus figuratively are hair raising. *Breeze* opens with a sax unison atop a tram choir which then is augmented by the rest of the section. Diz and Kenny Hagood split vocal bop phrases through the following chorus and the one thereafter, for the Gillespie trumpet is the fluid, driving variety with lustrous ideas and surety of execution in the difficult passages.

It's the kind of inspired Diz you like to hear. The only weak part of the side is the alto chorus which doesn't quite jell and is unflatteringly spotlighted by the spaces left in a jerky rhythm pattern. **(Victor 20-3023)**

Thursday 23 September 1948

Dizzy Gillespie Orchestra close at the Regal Theatre in Chicago.

Sunday 26 September 1948

Dizzy Gillespie Orchestra play a dance at the Pershing Ballroom in Chicago. Charlie Parker guests with the band and a private recording is made.

CHARLIE PARKER (alto sax), DIZZY GILLESPIE, DAVE BURNS, WILLIE COOK, ELMON WRIGHT (trumpets); JESSE TARRANT, ANDY DURYEA (trombones); JOHN BROWN, ERNIE HENRY (alto sax); JOE GAYLES, JAMES MOODY (tenor sax); CECIL PAYNE (baritone sax); JAMES FOREMAN JR (piano); NELSON BOYD (bass); TEDDY STEWART (drums); CHANO POZO (conga)

Things To Come / Oo-Bop-Sh-Bam / Yesterdays / Night In Tunisia / Round Midnight / Good Bait / What Is This Thing Called Love? / Manteca / Algo Bueno / Lover Man / Unknown Blues / Don't Blame Me / I Can't Get Started / Groovin' High / Ool Ya Koo / All The Things You Are

Thursday 30 September 1948

Dizzy Gillespie Orchestra opens the fall season with a two-week engagement at the Royal Roost in New York City. Also on the bill are Anita O'Day and Tadd Dameron's Band.

Improved Dizzy Band Cuts Old To Shreds

New York—The Royal Roost continued its string of dynamite-charged attractions by following Count Basie with Dizzy Gillespie and his 15 pieces of bop, opening before the most enthusiastic audience to greet a group of performers since the spot began business. Dizzy gave his followers something to cheer about with an improved band that cut shreds out of the one with which he played the concert halls here last winter.

It even topped his recent performances at the Roost a few months ago.

Afro-Cuban music, featuring bongos, got heavy emphasis. A touch of commercialism was added to the performance by all members of the band to sell the customers whether they understood anything about bop or not.

Luminaries Turn Out

Diz was greeted on his return to Broadway by such persons as heavyweight champ Joe Louis, Sarah Vaughan, Benny Goodman, Russ Case, Johnny Long, Nellie Lutcher, Denny Dennis, Lou Bellson, Charlie Shavers, Henny Youngman, Fred Robbins, and George Frazier.

Beginning the second week of her three-week engagement, concluded by now, Anita O'Day shared marquee billing and worked with a rhythm section, from Tadd Dameron's bop outfit, with Lou Stein replacing Tadd at the keyboard.

Anita was better prepared than at her opening when she was delayed en route and arrived after the evening's performance had started, thereby missing any chance for rehearsal.

Stein turned in a commendable job at the piano, ad libbing that night, and continued shining on the night of Diz's preem.

It can be assumed from a few stage-whispered remarks during her second week that Anita wasn't too happy with New York. She'd shine better with full band accompaniment, especially in view of the brassiness of the Gillespie outfit, to which the audience had become accustomed by the time the bop songbird came on.

Cramped in Spot

Anita still sings fine, has good delivery and is just as capable of selling out as in the days when she let herself go in front of the Krupa band. She complains that she's cramped working in the confines of a small spotlight and prefers bright lights, which is more in keeping with her usual presentation.

Perhaps Miss O'Day knows a thing or two about how she should be presented, for, with the house lights down, the customers weren't exactly overpolite to her performance.

Saturday 2 October 1948

Dizzy Gillespie Orchestra broadcast from the Royal Roost in New York City.

DIZZY GILLESPIE, DAVE BURNS, WILLIE COOK, ELMON WRIGHT (trumpets); JESSE TARRANT, ANDY DURYEA (trombones); JOHN BROWN, ERNIE HENRY (alto sax); JOE GAYLES, JAMES MOODY (tenor sax); CECIL PAYNE (baritone sax); JAMES FOREMAN JR (piano); NELSON BOYD (bass); TEDDY STEWART (drums); CHANO POZO (conga); JOHNNY HARTMAN (vocal)

Relaxin' At Camarillo / Things To Come / Soulphony In Three Hearts / One Bass Hit / I Should Care (vJH) */ Guarachi Guaro / Oop-Pop-A-Da / I Waited For You* (theme)

Tuesday 5 October 1948

Dizzy Gillespie Orchestra broadcast from the Royal Roost in New York City.

DIZZY GILLESPIE, DAVE BURNS, WILLIE COOK, ELMON WRIGHT (trumpets); JESSE TARRANT, ANDY DURYEA (trombones); JOHN BROWN, ERNIE HENRY (alto sax); JOE GAYLES, JAMES MOODY (tenor sax); CECIL PAYNE (baritone sax); JAMES FOREMAN JR (piano); NELSON BOYD (bass); TEDDY STEWART (drums); CHANO POZO (conga)

The Squirrel / Enchantment (Katy) / Taboo / Confess / Oop-Pop-A-Da (vDG, JB)

Dizzy at the Royal Roost with (clockwise from top left): Ray McKinley, Stan Kenton, Woody herman, Buddy Rich, disc jockeys Bill Williams, Fred Robbins and Symphony Sid, Stan Kenton and June Christy.

Saturday 9 October 1948

Dizzy Gillespie Orchestra broadcast from the Royal Roost in New York City.

DIZZY GILLESPIE, DAVE BURNS, WILLIE COOK, ELMON WRIGHT (trumpets); JESSE TARRANT, ANDY DURYEA (trombones); JOHN BROWN, ERNIE HENRY (alto sax); JOE GAYLES, JAMES MOODY (tenor sax); CECIL PAYNE (baritone sax); JAMES FOREMAN JR (piano); NELSON BOYD (bass); TEDDY STEWART (drums); CHANO POZO (conga); JOHNNY HARTMAN (vocal)

Lady Bird / Our Delight / Enchantment / But Beautiful / One Bass Hit / Manteca / Good Bait / Day By Day (vJH) */ S'posin'* (vJH) */ Groovin' High*

Saturday 16 October 1948

Dizzy Gillespie Orchestra broadcast from the Royal Roost in New York City.

DIZZY GILLESPIE, DAVE BURNS, WILLIE COOK, ELMON WRIGHT (trumpets); JESSE TARRANT, ANDY DURYEA (trombones); JOHN BROWN, ERNIE HENRY (alto sax); JOE GAYLES, JAMES MOODY (tenor sax); CECIL PAYNE (baritone sax); JAMES FOREMAN JR (piano); NELSON BOYD (bass); TEDDY STEWART (drums); CHANO POZO (conga); JOHNNY HARTMAN (vocal)

Ow! / *Day By Day* (vJH) / *Two Bass Hit* / *Confess* (vJH) / *Groovin' High* / *Oop-Pop-A-Da* (vDG, JB) / *Ray's Idea* / *S'posin'* (vJH) / *Guarachi Guaro* / *On The Bongo Beat*

The House that
Bop Built...

NIGHTLY CONCERTS OF PROGRESSIVE JAZZ

Produced by MONTE KAY
Staged by ALBERT CARLO
Publicity by MIKE HALL

●

Bill and Ralph's

Royal Roost

"Metropolitan Bopera House"

Broadway, at 47th Street, N.Y.

Thursday 21 October 1948

Dizzy Gillespie's 31st birthday.

Saturday 23 October 1948

Dizzy Gillespie Orchestra broadcast from the Royal Roost in New York City.

DIZZY GILLESPIE, DAVE BURNS, WILLIE COOK, ELMON WRIGHT (trumpets); JESSE TARRANT, ANDY DURYEA (trombones); JOHN BROWN, ERNIE HENRY (alto sax); JOE GAYLES, JAMES MOODY (tenor sax); CECIL PAYNE (baritone sax); JAMES FOREMAN JR (piano); NELSON BOYD (bass); TEDDY STEWART (drums); CHANO POZO (conga); JOHNNY HARTMAN, DINAH WASHINGTON (vocal)

I Can't Get Started / *More Than You Know* (vJH) / *Ow!* / *That Old Black Magic* (vJH) / *Manteca* / *Emanon* / *Ray's Idea* / *Guarachi Guaro* / *Confess* (vJH) / *Stay On It* / *S'posin'* (vJH) / *Cool Breeze* / *Evil Gal Blues* (vDW) / *Stairway To The Stars* (vDW)

Sunday 24 October 1948

Dizzy Gillespie trumpeter Dave Burns marries Audrey Dillard in New York City.

Wednesday 27 October 1948

Dizzy Gillespie Orchestra close at the Royal Roost in New York City.

DOWN BEAT

VOL. 15—NO. 23

CHICAGO, NOVEMBER 17, 1948

(Copyright, 1948, Down Beat Publishing Co.)

'Learn Everything-- Rudiments On Up!' Dizzy Warns Kids

By JACK EGAN

New York—Dizzy's in a dither. Not anything personal. Or his band, for that going along fine, better than ever. It's Professor Gillespie. "Too many people lark," moans the Diz. "Sure, it's creating a lot of excitement. There's a lot of publicity about it and it's doing us lots of good at the box office. But too many kids studying music are letting it blind them.

"Some other leaders have pointed out the same thing. If the kids get so hip they frown on everything that isn't out-and-out bop, we're going to wind up with a sad bunch of musicians ten years from now.

"They have to learn all the rudiments, just as the rest of us did. When I was growing up, all I wanted to play was swing, but I had to learn the other stuff, too. It's a good thing for Dizzy Gillespie and his present position that I did.

"Eldridge was my boy. All I ever did was try to play like him but I...

Franz Lehar Dies Of Cancer At 78

Vienna — Franz Lehar, composer of *The Merry Widow*, died of cancer at his summer home near here October 24 at the age of 78. He had been ill for two years.

Lehar, whose father was a military bandmaster, joined the army of the Austro-Hungarian empire in 1890 and for 12 years conducted army bands. Three and a half years after his resignation from the army his most famous operetta *The Merry Widow* had its first performance in Vienna. That was on December 30, 1905.

Among his other compositions were ...

APOLLO
HARLEM'S HIGH SPOT

"THE KING OF BE-BOP"

ONE WEEK ONLY
BEG. FRI., OCT. 29th

DIZZY GILLESPIE

His BAND and REVUE

The Newest Singing Sensation

RUTH BROWN

THE WONG SISTERS

HARRIS AND SCOTT

WED. NITE: AMATEURS

SAT. MIDNIGHT SHOW

Friday 29 October 1948

Dizzy Gillespie Orchestra open a one-week engagement at the Apollo Theatre in New York City. Also on the bill are Ruth Brown, The Wong Sisters and Harris & Scott.

Thursday 4 November 1948

Dizzy Gillespie Orchestra close at the Apollo Theatre in New York City.

Friday 5 November 1948

Dizzy Gillespie Orchestra play a concert at Cornell University.

DIZZY GILLESPIE, DAVE BURNS, WILLIE COOK, ELMON WRIGHT (trumpets); JESSE TARRANT, ANDY DURYEA (trombones); JOHN BROWN, ERNIE HENRY (alto sax); JOE GAYLES, JAMES MOODY (tenor sax); CECIL PAYNE (baritone sax); JAMES FOREMAN JR (piano); NELSON BOYD (bass); TEDDY STEWART (drums); CHANO POZO (conga); JOHNNY HARTMAN (vocal)

Duff Capers / *Nyeche* / *Tabu* / *They Say It's Wonderful* (vJH) / *Ool-Ya-Koo* / *'Round Midnight* / *Stay On It* / *Ow!* / *Manteca* / *Guarachi Guaro* / *I Should Care* (vJH) / *Afro Cuban Drum Suite* / *Lilette* (vJH) / *S'posin'* (vJH) / *Swedish Suite* / *Groovin' High* / *Soulphony In Three Hearts* / *Oop-Pop-A-Da* / *Theme*

Wednesday 17 November 1948

Dizzy Gillespie Orchestra play a one-nighter in Columbia, South Carolina.

Thursday 18 November 1948

Dizzy Gillespie Orchestra play a one-nighter in New Bern, North Carolina.

Friday 19 November 1948

Dizzy Gillespie Orchestra play a one-nighter in Henderson, North Carolina.

Saturday 20 November 1948

Dizzy Gillespie Orchestra play a one-nighter in Charleston, West Virginia.

Sunday 21 November 1948

Dizzy Gillespie Orchestra play a one-nighter in Ronceverte, West Virginia.

Monday 22 November 1948

Dizzy Gillespie Orchestra play a one-nighter in Raleigh, North Carolina.

Tuesday 23 November 1948

Dizzy Gillespie Orchestra play a one-nighter in Danville, Virginia.

Wednesday 24 November 1948

Dizzy Gillespie Orchestra play a one-nighter in Timmonsville, South Carolina.

Thursday 25 November 1948

Dizzy Gillespie Orchestra play a one-nighter in Greensboro, North Carolina.

Friday 26 November 1948

Dizzy Gillespie Orchestra play a one-nighter in Roanoke, Virginia.

Monday 29 November 1948

Dizzy Gillespie Orchestra play a one-nighter in Atlanta, Georgia.

Wednesday 1 December 1948

Dizzy Gillespie Orchestra play a one-nighter in New Orleans, Louisiana.

Down Beat reviews Dizzy's latest Victor release:

Dizzy Gillespie
*** *Minor Walk*
*** *Algo Bueno*

If Victor has a sizable stockpile of Dizzy's big band wax of the quality of the last two releases, it should be prosecuted for discrimination against boppers for ladling it out in such picayunish doses.

As a matter of fact, Victor execs should be censored anyhow for not having devoted at least as much engineering talent to recording this great band as they lavish on, say, a Tony Martin. Admittedly, with all that goes on in the Gillespie band, it takes a lot of doing to get it down properly, but the casual manner in which the band now is waxed makes for a loss of effect that could be sensational in some spots where all that comes out now is a vague roar as section against section clamors for attention.

Technically, Victor is one of the best in getting the right sound from almost any group of instruments, but it drops the ball when it comes to getting the most from big band progressive jazz of the style of this band. *Minor* is a screamer but not without change of pace as in the switch from ensemble to piano after the opener. Diz' full chorus is wonderful, and the following alto chorus on top of the same background is well worth attention, too.

Algo was penned by Dizzy and, along with its running mate, utilizes the tremendously rhythmic Afro-Cuban beat that is used on most of his current bop. Here, also, is more fine trumpet, a flash of excellent alto followed by heavy ensemble. It, more than *Minor*, requires a number of listenings due to its super-complex content. (**Victor 20-3186**)

Thursday 2 December 1948

Dizzy Gillespie Orchestra play a one-nighter in Jackson, Mississippi.

Chano Pozo (28), who has returned to New York after his drums are stolen, is shot dead in a bar in Harlem.

Dizzy Gillespie Drummer Shot In Tavern

NEW YORK—Members and followers of the entertainment world were shocked when they learned that Chano Pozo, rated as one of the nation's greatest bongo drummers, was shot and instantly killed Thursday night while drinking at the Rio Bar on Lenox Avenue at 111th Street.

Rumor had it that the incident that led to the slaying was an argument over narcotics. This angle has not been confirmed by the Police Department.

For the past eighteen months, and until his untimely death, Pozo was a member of the Dizzy Gillespie Band. He composed several tunes, his latest, "Manteca," and "Cubana Be–Cubana Bop."

Friday 3 December 1948

Dizzy Gillespie Orchestra open a week-end engagement at the W. C. Fields Theatre in Memphis, Tennessee.

Monday 6 December 1948

Dizzy Gillespie Orchestra close in Memphis, Tennessee.

Thursday 9 December 1948

Dizzy Gillespie Orchestra open a two-week engagement at the Strand Theatre in New York City. Bop vocalist Joe Carroll debuts with the band. Sharing the bill are Maxine Sullivan, The Deep River Boys and the Berry Brothers. The film presentation is 'The Decision of Christopher Blake' starring Alexis Smith and Robert Douglas.

New York—Bop's number one salesman, Dizzy Gillespie, did right by his product in selling it to the public on his first downtown theater engagement at the Strand.

In a show top heavy with other acts (six, including the male singer), Diz and his band came through to panic the house with his bop specialties, broke it up with *Manteca*, and killed 'em with *Oopapada*, the latter serving as the finale.

On this he featured Joe Carroll, an outstanding bop singer, then at the end was joined by the dancing Berry Brothers for a bop vocal chorus, after which the entire company—Maxine Sullivan, Deep River Boys, Spider Bruce, et al—joined in the singing of a final chorus.

The Diz lived up to all expectations as a showman, and his band delivered its wares in an amusing and capable manner. Too bad the show, which ran 70 minutes when caught, was so overloaded with other acts.

Thursday 23 December 1948

Dizzy Gillespie Orchestra close at the Strand Theatre in New York City.

Saturday 25 December 1948
Dizzy Gillespie Orchestra appear in a Christmas night concert at Carnegie Hall in New York City. Charlie Parker is also on the bill.

DJs, Diz' Humor (?), Plus Other Mess Mar Concert

By MICHAEL LEVIN

New York—The following intersting events took place at Dizzy Gillespie's 105-minute Christmas night concert in Carnegie Hall:

● Sabu Martinez, billed as a conga drummer, walked on stage with a set of bongos, had to borrow a chair from a spectator seated on stage, and promptly broke one of the drums in his first 30 seconds of playing.

● Disc jockey Symphony Sid, co-sponsor of the event with fellow wax horseman Leonard Feather, got in three separate plugs for one of *his* sponsors, Music Hall Crown Jewelers.

● Dizzy introduced a friend, creator of "those mad bop ties the band is wearing," announced free ties would be given away. They were at program's end, making a slight shambles out of the formal conclusion.

● During guest Sarah Vaughan's spot, a small emissary brought in the music for tenor man Budd Johnson's part.

● A group of Brooklyn boppists, seated in a box, were just as drunkenly loud as their 1938 forebearers, managed to clap the wrong beats just as effusively.

● Local platter pilotician Feather made 28 flurried journeys on and off-stage, dead-heated Gillespie several times at the mike, went through a most splendiferous introduction of Symphony Sid (who was to introduce a group of poll winners) only to have winner Tadd Dameron walk on instead of Sid.

● Some agent should have received 10 per cent for the behatted and coat-carrying crew which constantly circulated back of the band on stage. The entire scene looked a little like Forty Thieves in Search of Ali Baba.

The above items are not presented merely facetiously. Both Feather and Torin have complained vigorously about the slap-dash manner in which some jazz concerts here have been staged. It seems they should have applied some of their own critical experience to what was too often a rhythmic clambake.

More Extraneous Matter

Outside of such other frivolities as the last part of the Ventura group's numbers being spent with Feather and the Carnegie hall representative pointing to wrist watches and apparently arguing vociferously, the major presentation defect was the band's seating.

The Ellington concert here proved conclusively that a jazz band to be heard satisfactorily in Carnegie hall must be tiered. Nobody bothered to do this with Gillespie, the result was once more the old familiar hash. Reeds were lost in brass clamor, rhythm sounded tubby and colorless.

Musically the highlights of the 21 numbers were Charlie Parker's short stint with the poll-winning all-star combo, *Manteca* with Martinez and Joe Harris added on timbales for a rocking Latin rhythm section, John Lewis' well-conceived *Period Suite*, Tadd Dameron's serious wrestle with changing emotional patterns in *Soulphony*, Sarah Vaughan's *Lover Man* and the well-balanced sound maintained by the Ventura combo.

Altoman Ernie Henry and tenorist Johnson were the standout soloists of the Gillespie crew, with baritone Cecil Payne's bad tone negating many of the things he did get off.

Eckstine Imitator

Vocalist Johnny Hartman is proof again of the fact that Billy Eckstine should be the biggest male singer in the country commercially. Heaven knows, enough singers try to sound like him.

Drummer Teddy Stewart, like Ellingtonite Sonny Greer, should stand as ample warnings to all followers: you must muffle a bass drum in Carnegie, lest it sound like an unleashed tuba section.

Comedy touches were supplied by Joe Carroll's clever vobopping on *Oopapada* including some fine takeoffs on Bing, *Holidays for Strings*, *The Whistler*, Illinois Jacquet's squealings, and Ella Fitzgerald. The bop format, by the way, of a necessary formal coda return to the original phrase often can be a dramatic letdown, certainly was here.

Dizzy continued his attempts to be the only clown who actually plays an instrument. Sometimes the touches were successful: in *Sposin'*, the trams upped and downed without playing to a laugh from the crowd, while the interpolation of *Sabre Dance* in the frenetic *Manteca* was aptly funny and a satirical commentary at the same time.

Too often, however, Diz's hip shufflings, leg tremors, and hand gestures merely transgress and are vulgar rather than amusing. He has much to learn about timing and taste if he wishes to be a comic.

His playing was better than it often has been at these concerts with fuller tone and less pressing for ideas. Parker, however, with his genuine musical ebullience of ideas and apparent effortlessness in getting them out, set him off with ease.

Good Blend

The band itself blended better and sounded more organized than it has in the past. It still, however, would be nice to have the reeds completely in tune and the brass reading together, as well as a little more attention to playing softly once in a while.

This could have been a much better concert with a little more attention to detail by Gillespie and producers Feather and Torin. The virtual sellout crowd on a brutally cold night proves once again that despite the boppists' failings, they are offering a feeling of something different and vital which attracts the younger crowd. Knowing this, they should take care to make something out of the opportunity given them.

Wednesday 29 December 1948
Dizzy Gillespie Orchestra record for Victor in New York City.
DIZZY GILLESPIE, DAVE BURNS, WILLIE COOK, ELMON WRIGHT (trumpets); JESSE TARRANT, ANDY DURYEA, SAM HURT (trombones); JOHN BROWN, ERNIE HENRY (alto sax); JOE GAYLES, BUDD JOHNSON (tenor sax); CECIL PAYNE (baritone sax); JAMES FOREMAN JR (piano); AL MCKIBBON (bass); TEDDY STEWART (drums); JOE HARRIS (conga); SABU MARTINEZ (bongo)
Guarachi Guaro / Duff Capers / Lover Come Back To Me / I'm Be Boppin' Too (vDG, 2 takes)

Friday 31 December 1948
Dizzy Gillespie Orchestra play a one-nighter in Johnson City, New York.

1949

Saturday 1 January 1949

Dizzy Gillespie Orchestra play a one-nighter in Cleveland, Ohio.

Sunday 2 January 1949

Dizzy Gillespie Orchestra play an afternoon concert at the Civic Opera House in Chicago. The band head for the west coast while Dizzy returns to New York.

Monday 3 January 1949

Dizzy takes part in the Metronome All Stars recording session in New York City.

DIZZY GILLESPIE, MILES DAVIS, FATS NAVARRO (trumpets); J. J. JOHNSON, KAI WINDING (trombones); BUDDY DE FRANCO (clarinet); CHARLIE PARKER (alto sax); CHARLIE VENTURA (tenor sax); ERNIE CACERES (baritone sax); LENNIE TRISTANO (piano); BILLY BAUER (guitar); EDDIE SAFRANSKI (bass); SHELLY MANNE (drums); PETE RUGOLO (director)

Overtime (2 takes) / *Victory Ball* (3 takes)

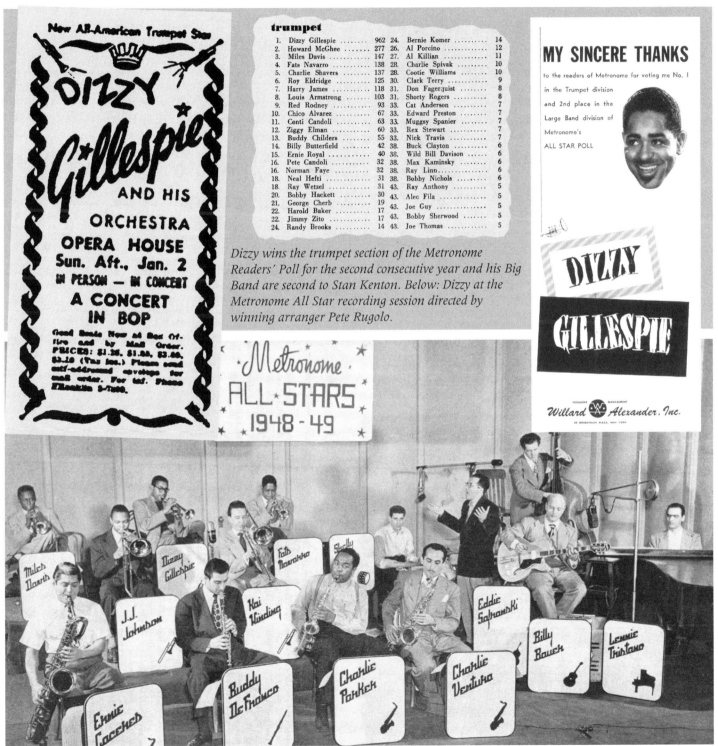

trumpet

1.	Dizzy Gillespie	962	24.	Bernie Komer	14
2.	Howard McGhee	277	26.	Al Porcino	12
3.	Miles Davis	147	27.	Al Killian	11
4.	Fats Navarro	138	28.	Charlie Spivak	10
5.	Charlie Shavers	137	28.	Cootie Williams	10
6.	Roy Eldridge	125	30.	Clark Terry	9
7.	Harry James	118	31.	Don Fagerquist	8
8.	Louis Armstrong	103	31.	Shorty Rogers	8
9.	Red Rodney	93	33.	Cat Anderson	7
10.	Chico Alvarez	67	33.	Edward Preston	7
11.	Conti Candoli	63	33.	Muggsy Spanier	7
12.	Ziggy Elman	60	33.	Rex Stewart	7
13.	Buddy Childers	55	33.	Nick Travis	7
14.	Billy Butterfield	42	38.	Buck Clayton	6
15.	Ernie Royal	40	38.	Wild Bill Davison	6
16.	Pete Candoli	32	38.	Max Kaminsky	6
16.	Norman Faye	32	38.	Ray Linn	6
18.	Neal Hefti	31	38.	Bobby Nichols	6
18.	Ray Wetzel	31	43.	Ray Anthony	5
20.	Bobby Hackett	30	43.	Alec Fila	5
21.	George Cherb	19	43.	Joe Guy	5
22.	Harold Baker	17	43.	Bobby Sherwood	5
22.	Jimmy Zito	17	43.	Joe Thomas	5
24.	Randy Brooks	14			

MY SINCERE THANKS

to the readers of Metronome for voting me No. 1 in the Trumpet division and 2nd place in the Large Band division of Metronome's ALL STAR POLL

Willard Alexander, Inc.

Dizzy wins the trumpet section of the Metronome Readers' Poll for the second consecutive year and his Big Band are second to Stan Kenton. Below: Dizzy at the Metronome All Star recording session directed by winning arranger Pete Rugolo.

Wednesday 5 January 1949

Dizzy Gillespie Orchestra are scheduled to play a one-nighter at the Coconut Grove in Salt Lake City. A heavy snow prevents the band from making it but Dizzy is already there and makes the date with the stranded Woody Herman Band.

Real Cool, But Diz' Band Gone

Salt Lake City—The great snowfall which tied up much of the west recently managed to strand Woody Herman's band here, when it had a date in Denver, and keep Dizzy Gillespie's boys from reaching town in time for their appearance at the Coconut Grove. So Herman's Herd, with the Diz sitting in, played the Grove, jampacked in spite of the weather. Photo above shows Gillespie, disc jockey Al (Jazzbo) Collins, Herman, and Herman vibist Terry Gibbs.

Friday 7 January 1949

Dizzy Gillespie Orchestra play a one-nighter in Sacramento, California.

Saturday 8 January 1949

Dizzy Gillespie Orchestra play a one-nighter in Stockton, California.

Sunday 9 January 1949

Dizzy Gillespie Orchestra play a one-nighter at the Edgewater Beach ballroom in San Francisco, California.

Diz Cracks S. F. Mark; Back In Spring

San Francisco—After playing two dates here in mid-January, Dizzy Gillespie was all set to return again on March 10 to open for two weeks at Cafe Society Uptown at a sum reported "better than $2,500 a week." But bookings got snarled up, and the deal fell through at press time, with Diz not returning until late spring. The Cafe, however, had Charlie Ventura's combo tentatively set to open the 10th.

Diz, nevertheless, practically broke up television in this area when he made his west coast TV debut over KPIX with the Vernon Alley trio. And Diz did break all recent records at the Edgewater Beach ballroom, outdrawing such bands as Kenton, Herman, Rich, Krupa, Ellington, and Hampton, as an estimated 2,400 attended on the coldest night in 12 years.

Although Ellis Levey, owner of the spot, refused to divulge any definite figures, it was reliably reported that the crowd, which packed the dance floor and the balconies, numbered at least 2,400.

Diz' other date here, at Oakland the following night, was not so well-attended. The Fourth Estaters, headed by Paul Green, promoted both dates.

The Bay area dates following the frantic week for the band were reported in the last Beat. New road manager Paul Parker earned plenty of praise for getting the band to California through the blizzard.

Band played without music and on borrowed instruments the first night, but these arrived in time for the Oakland date and the subsequent concert in Los Angeles two days later. _____ —rjg

Monday 10 January 1949

Dizzy Gillespie Orchestra play a one-nighter in Oakland, California.

Dizzy also appears on Jimmy Lyons' KNBC music quiz show *Disc and Data*. Other guests on the show are French singer Jean Sablon, Vernon Alley and Ralph Gleason.

Wednesday 12 January 1949

Dizzy Gillespie Orchestra play a concert at the Shrine Auditorium in Los Angeles.

DIZZY GILLESPIE, BENNY HARRIS, WILLIE COOK, ELMON WRIGHT (trumpets); JESSE TARRANT, ANDY DURYEA, SAM HURT (trombones); JOHN BROWN, ERNIE HENRY (alto sax); JOE GAYLES, YUSEF LATEEF (tenor sax); AL GIBSON (baritone sax); JAMES FOREMAN JR (piano); AL McKIBBON (bass); TEDDY STEWART (drums); VINCE GUERRO (conga); JOE CARROLL (vocal)
Guarachi Guaro / Soulphony In Three Hearts / Oop-Pop-A-Da (vJC, DG) / *I'm Be Boppin' Too* (vJC) / *Lover Come Back To Me / Algo Bueno / Good Bait / Ool-Ya-Koo* (vDG, JC)

Dizzy Gillespie Concert At Auditorium Was So-So

**By J. T. Gipson,
Sentinel Theatrical Editor**

Dizzy Gillespie, the High Priest of Be-Bop and his orchestra played to a near capacity crowd of 3500 Bop worshippers last week at the Shrine auditorium, and although a steady downpour persisted, the fabulous Diz had the crowd standing in a line nearly a block long for tickets.

The concert in itself wasn't anything in particular to write home about. It was the same old musical soup warmed over. Diz played the usual recordings which made him famous. Only, at the Shrine, you heard nearly three hours of Be-Bop. The Boppers loved it. Each number was played to as near perfection as a Be-Bop number can be. On some you recognized the selection being played. On others the music sounded like a wreck between a truckload of Hogs and a truck.. loaded.. with.. empty milk cans. But whatever the numbers sounded like, the Bop followers... ..and.. clamored.. for ... trumpeting ... high, hard, fast, flawless and clear horn. He makes a good appearance in front of a band. Handsome (in a Be-Bop'ish sort of way), and has a friendly personality. His band played together, but they played too loud.

In band vocalist Johnny Hartman, Dizzy literally has a gold mine. This tall, handsome bashful lad is talented. He's the one singer around today who doesn't try to imitate Billy Eckstine, thank goodness! He sounds original, and good.

You don't realize what a really great ballad style he has until you hear him tour with torchants. On swing numbers, his singing sounded n.s.g.. but on ballads—love that man!

Rose Murphy, the Chi-Chi girl, lived up to all advance publicity on her. She has a shy style of toying with the piano,.. and.. her.. baby-voiced lyrics is a musical treat. Her piano-pounding and clap-clap rhythm is music to.. the.. ears... She played several numbers, and had to beg off.

Main flaw in the concert was the rowdiness of a few of Dizzy's jitterbug fans who staged a near-riot jumping on the stage at the start of the concert. Policemen were called to hold the over-enthusiastic crowd of buggish little boppers back.

Gene Norman, a disc jockey, added to his bankroll as sponsor of the event.

SUCCESSFUL CAREERS IN MUSIC

Copyright, 1949, Martin Band Instrument Co., Elkhart, Indiana

The story of trumpeter DIZZY GILLESPIE outstanding Martin artist

This is the true life story of a famous American musician . . . published by the Martin Band Instrument Company in tribute to his artistry and to the high standards of music education in America which made his career possible. Reprints for school bulletin boards available on request, from Martin or your Martin dealer.

1 John Birks Gillespie, better known today as "Dizzy," began his career with an instrument furnished by his school band. A neighbor loaned him a trumpet so he could practice at home.

2 Born in Cheraw, S. C., Dizzy got most of his formal education in Philadelphia, where he was recognized as an outstanding member of his high school band.

3 Long hours of practice paid off when Frank Fairfax listened and liked his playing. He gave 18-year-old Dizzy a job . . . the beginning of a professional career that was to bring him fame.

4 After playing two years with Fairfax, Gillespie joined Teddy Hill's band, which toured England and the Continent . . . receiving an enthusiastic welcome from European jazz fans.

5 When he returned from overseas, Dizzy decided he needed a horn on which he could play his very best. After a careful trial of leading makes, he selected his first Martin.

6 Dizzy, during the early 1940's played in a group at Minton's Playhouse in New York where he and a few others created a new type of jazz that was to become known as "bebop."

7 The next several years he gained considerable recognition playing trumpet with Duke Ellington, Cab Calloway, Benny Carter, Charlie Barnet, Earl Hines, and other famous bands.

8 With Oscar Pettiford, Dizzy got together a small 52nd Street combo which lasted until 1946. Later he organized several small and large bands of his own.

9 Esquire magazine voted Gillespie its "New Star" award in 1945. Metronome's poll in 1947 acclaimed him top trumpeter in the land. Dizzy Gillespie, King of Bop, had arrived.

10 Like so many leading musicians, Dizzy is convinced that his Martin can't be beat, especially for recording. His fine trumpet work can be heard on records under many labels.

11 The marvelous technique of Diz with his Martin has made him the most copied trumpeter since Beiderbecke. His beret, glasses and tiny goatee have become the trade-mark of bop.

Thursday 13 January 1949
Dizzy Gillespie Orchestra open a three-week engagement at Billy Berg's in Los Angeles.

Sunday 23 January 1949
Dizzy Gillespie Orchestra play a benefit for Bud Scott at Paul Robbins Crickett Club in Los Angeles.

Wednesday 2 February 1949
Dizzy Gillespie Orchestra close at Billy Berg's in Los Angeles.

Dizzy also appears as a guest star at the Benevolent Variety Artists' 2nd Annual Barn Dance at the La Vada Ballroom in Los Angeles.

After closing at Billy Berg's, Dizzy and the Orchestra head for San Francisco for a series of Bay Area appearances.

BENEVOLENT
VARIETY ARTISTS'
2ND ANNUAL
BARN DANCE
LA VADA BALLROOM
249 East Vernon Avenue
Wednesday, Feb. 2nd, 1949
· · · · GUEST STARS · · · ·
DIZZY GILLESPIE
BILLY ECKSTINE
NELLIE LUTCHER
FREDDIE JAMES
MABEL SCOTT
WILLIE BEST
CHARLES BROWN
HERB JEFFRIES
&
HORACE HENDERSON
Admission 50c — 10 P.M. Until ?

Wednesday 16 February 1949
Dizzy Gillespie Orchestra close in San Francisco.

Friday 18 February 1949
Dizzy Gillespie Orchestra open a two-night engagement in Seattle.

Saturday 19 February 1949
Dizzy Gillespie Orchestra close in Seattle.

Sunday 20 February 1949
Dizzy Gillespie Orchestra open a three-night engagement in Portland, Oregon.

Tuesday 22 February 1949
Dizzy Gillespie Orchestra close in Portland, Oregon. Monday was a blacks only dance, Tuesday a whites only dance.

In Portland, Dizzy talks to *Down Beat's* Ted Hallock before moving on to Sacramento and Los Angeles

Dizzy Proves He's Tops In Showmanship Ability

By RALPH J. GLEASON
San Francisco—Dizzy Gillespie left the Bay area after a three-hour presentation which from the opening *Emanon* to the closing *Oopapada*, was one of the greatest evening's performances we've ever attended. From a musical standpoint, it's hard to conceive of a better concert, and from the standpoint of showmanship, it's even more difficult.

Aside from his superiority as a musician, he's one of the best of scene-stealer-band-leader-dancer-musical satirists.

We know his stage antics not always have proved acceptable to critics. We're sorry, but he kills us!

For sheer musical excitement, we doubt if any band ever has approached the fervour that Dizzy's group musters.

It played Gillespie standards such as *Ool-Ya-Koo*, *Manteca*, *Cool Breeze*, *Minor Walk*, *One Bass Hit*, *Swedish Suite*, and *Say Eh*. Joe Carroll and Dizzy had the audience limp. Sam Herd, Diz' fine young trombonist, even sang *The Blues* (to the tune of *Hand Fulla Gimme*), and Johnny Hartman had the gals swooning with his ballads.

Handing Out Praise
Special praise must be earmarked for Al McKibbon's fine bass work and excellent performances by altoists Ernie Henry and John Brown and the new tenor, Bill Evans, both singly and as a team.

And a special batch of praise should be given to Teddy Stewart. On number after number, his drive accounted for much of the excitement of the band, and his taste made him one of the most musical drummers we've ever heard.

Dizzy's New Idea Would Help Interpret Arrangers

Portland, Oregon—Dizzy Gillespie has an idea. A good one. A new one. One which should have been thought of long ago. Because his arrangements (and those played by other bop-conscious bands) require more "interpretation" than sight-reading prowess, Diz and/or his penners usually supervise personally first performances of new scores.

"The men play the notes through. They play them right. Which is fine. *Then* I tell them *how* to play the thing. Quarter-notes can remain just quarter-notes, or they can sound 'ooopa oo-pa'." This then is Gillespie's "idea."

"Why can't arrangers who send scores to travelling bands also record and send a personal description of how the arrangement should be played. The guy should sit down and describe the score, bar by bar. When we get the disc, we play it before we try the tune … with each man reading his part as the arranger tells us what he wants.

Right Flavor
"With an arranger I know, I can usually tell what he had in mind. But there are men I haven't worked with. This system would give everything we play the intended flavor. Now, when we return to the east, some arrangers don't recognise their scores."

Diz talked with this reporter during a dinner at Portland's Press club, where he spent an evening as guest of honor. "I hope to tour abroad again soon, I'd like to start with Italy. I don't have any hard feelings about Belgium, or about Carlos de Radzitsky. I like him, and want to return."

Gillespie said he was quoted correctly by *Time* in its recent feature article concerning Louis Armstrong. Diz added: "Louis is the plantation character that so many of us …younger men…resent." John Birks also commented bitterly on the fact that he had played two dances while here: a Monday night dance for colored persons only, and a Tuesday evening affair for all races.

Reverse English
"Many people told me Monday night that some Negroes had stayed away…resenting the reverse English discrimination." When told about Hazel Scott's recent attacks on bigotry in Pasco, Washington, and Texas, and asked why he (Diz) hadn't complained to the Portland ballroom op, Gillespie replied:

"Hazel Scott can afford to make an issue of it. She gets between $2,500 and $5,000 an appearance and is married to a congressman."

This reporter's reactions to the band: six brass sound like ten; *How High The Moon* is evidently not in the orchestra's repertoire, a phenomena of no mean import; the reed section is sloppy and doesn't care; be-bop can be, and is in this band, as repetitious as a recurring Lombardo riff; conga drummer Martinez is no Chano Pozo; no one wore a beret.

Tuesday 1 March 1949

Dizzy Gillespie Orchestra open a one-week engagement at the Million Dollar Theatre in Los Angeles.

Monday 7 March 1949

Dizzy Gillespie Orchestra close at the Million Dollar Theatre in Los Angeles.

Diz To Put Bop Touch To More Standard Tunes

San Francisco—Dizzy Gillespie plans to feature more bop variations on standard tunes in order to make his music more understandable to the average guy, the boppist told KQW's jockey Bob Goerner here during the latter's second anniversary week celebration which featured interviews with all the talent in the area.

"We're going to have the melody going along with some countermelodies so they can understand what we're doing," Diz said.

As to the future of bop, Diz told Goerner that in a few years it will be an amalgamation of two styles, so blended you won't be able to call it bop or Afro-Cuban.

It will be difficult for the latter to play bop, Diz said, and tough for the Americans to give out with authentic Cuban beats. He says he thinks that eventually it will be American playing the bop and Cubans the rhythms which will make it truly a music of the Americas.

Duke Ellington, in his interview, said in commenting on modern music: "Well, actually there's nothing new—modern harmony started back 100 years. The most desperately unmodern thing in the world is the repetition of one chord. The idea is to …"

MILLION DOLLAR

DOWNTOWN · BDWY. at 3rd
PHONE MICHIGAN 6272

NOW PLAYING
Duke Ellington
And His Orchestra

STARTING TUES., MAR. 1
New All-American Trumpet. Star

DIZZY Gillespie
AND HIS ORCHESTRA

Featuring

**Johnny Hartman
Joe Carroll**

Plus

Vaudeville Revue

FAREWELL DANCE

TUESDAY, MARCH 8

Avodon Ballroom

Featuring the Great

DIZZY GILLESPIE

HIGH PRIEST OF BE-BOP

This is Dizzy Gillespie's

Final California Appearance

Tuesday 8 March 1949

Dizzy Gillespie Orchestra play a Farewell Dance at the Avodon Ballroom in Los Angeles.

Friday 11 March 1949

Dizzy Gillespie Orchestra play a one-nighter in Denver, Colorado.

Saturday 12 March 1949

Dizzy Gillespie Orchestra play a one-nighter in Omaha, Nebraska.

Sunday 13 March 1949

Dizzy Gillespie Orchestra play a one-nighter in Rock Island, Illinois.

Monday 14 March 1949

Dizzy Gillespie Orchestra play a one-nighter in Indianapolis, Indiana.

Tuesday 15 March 1949

Dizzy Gillespie Orchestra play a one-nighter in South Bend, Indiana.

Wednesday 16 March 1949

Dizzy Gillespie Orchestra play a one-nighter in Milwaukee.

Friday 18 March 1949

Dizzy Gillespie Orchestra open a one-week engagement at the Regal Theatre in Chicago. Sarah Vaughan shares the billing.

REGAL
47th--South Parkway
FRIDAY, MARCH 18TH – ALL WEEK!
IN PERSON! ON STAGE!
DOUBLE - HEADLINER SHOW!
THE KING OF BE-BOP!

DIZZY GILLESPIE
AND HIS FAMOUS ORCHESTRA

FEATURING JOHNNY HARTMAN, JOE CARROLL—
HEAR THEM EXCLUSIVELY ON RCA-VICTOR RECORDS

CO-STARRED WITH MUSIC'S "NEW SOUND"
AMERICA'S TOP FEMALE SINGER! SONG STYLIST

SARAH VAUGHAN

WITH AN ALL-STAR STAGE JAMBOREE!

Featuring **JOHN (SPIDER BRUCE) MASON & COMPANY** And The

Sensational Dancer **RALPH BROWN**

—PLUS ROARING, THRILLING SCREEN ADVENTURE!—
MURDER ON HIGH! DARE DEVILS OF DERRICKS!

"MR. RECKLESS"
WILLIAM EYTHE - BARBARA BRITTON

Dizzy's Now A Real Gone Maracas Man

Chicago—Dizzy Gillespie plays a fine pair of maracas. The crowds that saw him here at the Regal theater may have wondered if the trumpet was only incidental, but, as Dizzy says, "these people want to be entertained, so we entertain them."

During the 1 1/4 hour show, Gillespie's horn could be heard on the opener, *Duff Capers*, and on *Say Eh*, where the Diz' trumpet sounded remarkably like a finger rubbed over wet glass. A marathon-length *Manteca*, Johnny Hartman's best concert tenor on *Old Man River*, and the Joe Carroll bop-and-innuendo specialty *Oopapada*, completed the band's solo work. Then they backed dancer Ralph Brown, the Spider Bruce comedy team, and singer Sarah Vaughan.

Sarah, hampered, as was the band, by a defective amplifying system, still sounded far better than any of her contemporaries, with a range, flexibility, and tone none of them can touch. She habitually leaves Regal audiences lukewarm, however—something perhaps smarter gowning might alleviate. Why she insists on looking like she's in a cocoon with a bustle is hardly understandable.

Gillespie's band backed her beautifully on the Sarah standards *I Cried For You, It's Magic, I Get A Kick Out Of You*, and *Everything I Have Is Yours*.

Having left conga drummer Sabu Martinez on the west coast, the maracas-wielding Dizzy had the following men with him: trumpets—Benny Harris, Willie Cook, Elmon Wright; saxes—Joe Gayles, Bill Evans (tenors), Ernie Henry, John Brown (altos), and Al Gibson (baritone); trombones—Rip Tarrant, Sam Hurt, Andy Duryea; rhythm—Jimmy Forman, piano, Al McKibbon, bass, and Teddy Stewart, drums.

They will, when they get to New York's Bop City, and, May 2, when they open at Chicago's Blue Note, cut the showmanship down a bit, Dizzy promised, and that we're waiting to see.

Thursday 24 March 1949
Dizzy Gillespie Orchestra close at the Regal Theatre in Chicago.

Friday 25 March 1949
Dizzy Gillespie Orchestra play a one-nighter in Louisville, Kentucky.

Saturday 26 March 1949
Dizzy Gillespie Orchestra play a one-nighter in Cincinnati, Ohio.

Sunday 27 March 1949
Dizzy Gillespie Orchestra play a one-nighter in Toledo, Ohio.

Monday 28 March 1949
Dizzy Gillespie Orchestra play a one-nighter in Columbus, Ohio.

Tuesday 29 March 1949
Dizzy Gillespie Orchestra play a one-nighter in Cleveland, Ohio.

Wednesday 30 March 1949
Dizzy Gillespie Orchestra play a one-nighter at the Savoy Ballroom in Pittsburgh, Pennsylvania.

Dizzy Postpones

New York—Dizzy Gillespie, originally set to return to the Royal Roost March 31, has postponed it until June.

Friday 1 April 1949
Dizzy Gillespie Orchestra open a one-week engagement at the Howard Theatre in Washington, D.C.

Thursday 7 April 1949
Dizzy Gillespie Orchestra close at the Howard Theatre in Washington, D.C.

Sunday 10 April 1949
Dizzy Gillespie Orchestra play a one-nighter at the Masonic Auditorium in Cleveland, Ohio.

Thursday 14 April 1949
Dizzy Gillespie Orchestra record for Victor in Chicago.
DIZZY GILLESPIE, BENNY HARRIS, WILLIE COOK, ELMON WRIGHT (trumpets); JESSE TARRANT, ANDY DURYEA, SAM HURT (trombones); JOHN BROWN, ERNIE HENRY (alto sax); JOE GAYLES, YUSEF LATEEF (tenor sax); AL GIBSON (baritone sax); JAMES FOREMAN JR (piano); AL McKIBBON (bass); TEDDY STEWART (drums); VINCE GUERRO (conga); JOHNNY HARTMAN, JOE CARROLL (vocal)
Swedish Suite / St. Louis Blues / I Should Care (vJH) / *That Old Black Magic* (vJH)

Friday 22 April 1949
Down Beat reviews Dizzy's latest Victor release:

Dizzy Gillespie
** *Lover Come Back To Me*
** *Guarachi Guaro*

Dizzy's postban wax is disappointing to these ears. *Lover* is an Afro-Cuban version of the Romberg tune with Diz playing a fairly straight out-of-meter chorus for a good deal longer than he should. The background is interesting but not enough to sustain interest until he finally breaks it up toward the end which, incidentally, drags out interminably.

Guaro is more of the same only with an altered guaracha beat something on the order of a slower *Manteca*. Here again the rhythm and orchestration are fairly interesting, but Diz does little of any note, and the Afro chant and gang shouting midway are tame.

And while we're on the subject, a repetitive bop lick such as the one gradually built up in volume through the last third of the record can get just as deadly and monotonous as an old Casa Loma riffer. **(Victor 20-3370)**

April's *Metronome* reviews the same release:

dizzy gillespie
Lover Come Back To Me C+
Guarachi Guaro C+

Diz has gone latin. He's also gone flat. His version of the old show tune might have come off if he had played better horn, but he didn't and the result sounds like just another Gillespie imitator. The reverse, which spots some better Dizzy horn, also employs a Latin rhythm section and, what with the poor sax intonation, could have been played by any relief band but is certainly not worthy of the great Gillespie aggregation to which we have become accustomed. (Victor 20-3370)

Monday 2 May 1949
Dizzy Gillespie Orchestra open a three-week engagement at the Blue Note in Chicago.

Friday 6 May 1949
Dizzy Gillespie Orchestra record for Victor in Chicago.
DIZZY GILLESPIE, BENNY HARRIS, WILLIE COOK, ELMON WRIGHT (trumpets); JESSE TARRANT, ANDY DURYEA, SAM HURT (trombones); JOHN BROWN, ERNIE HENRY (alto sax); JOE GAYLES, YUSEF LATEEF (tenor sax); AL GIBSON (baritone sax); JAMES FOREMAN JR (piano); AL McKIBBON (bass); TEDDY STEWART (drums); VINCE GUERRO (conga); JOE CARROLL (vocal)
Dizzier And Dizzier / Jump Did-Le Ba (vDG, JC) / *You Go To My Head* (vJH)

Dizzy Bop Blast Raises Ceiling Of Cellar Note

Chicago—One of the most talked-about bands, and the least-often pictured, Dizzy Gillespie's cabal is shown above as it appeared at the Blue Note here recently. Saxes are, from the left, Joe Gayles, Ernie Henry, John Brown (hidden by Gillespie), and Bill Evans. Baritone saxist Al Gibson didn't get within camera range. Teddy Stewart is on drums, and trum- pets are Benny Harris, Willie Cook, and **Elmon** Wright. Trombones you can see are Rip Tarrant **and** Sam Hurt, with Andy Duryea blocked out. Part of conga drummer Chappotin's head can be seen be- hind Gayles, while bassist Al McKibbon and **pianist** Jimmy Forman are out of the frame, too. So is **the** small set of drums Diz plays occasionally.

Dizzy Fails To Draw As Expected In 3-Week Stay

Chicago—Dizzy Gillespie's first location date in Chicago, three weeks at the Blue Note preceding the current Charlie Ventura run, didn't quite have them hanging from the rafters, although it was better business than the Note has seen in a number of weeks. Most local musicians got around to hearing Dizzy at least once, but they know how to nurse a bottle of beer as well as any teen-ager can a coke. And the expected mobbing just didn't happen.

The business of how much beer some spot sold, and how many persons showed up to buy it, may seem crass and unnecessary to the lovers of pure jazz and good music. But musicians aren't hired by clubs and saloons unless they bring enough business to justify their pay. Chicago has some fine local musicians, and numbers of others stop through from time to time.

Discouraged

But their current attitude is one of profound discouragement. There has been something of an exodus back to the farm, or the home town, or a turning to more stable ways to earn a living.

Even those havens of security, the radio stations, have done flip- flops recently in their haste to shuffle personnel to cut costs.

We could elaborate, but seems as if we did something like that last issue.

Dizzy did a fine job at the Note. Accent on comedy during the first few days diminished, and the band's early unevenness smoothed out. Dizzy's miming, especially of a Hampton-type tenor player during *Oopapada* (with Joe Carroll's sound effects), is almost art, of its type. The band has an enthusiasm that is engaging, a liveness that adds a great deal to their performance—in contrast to the pre-occupied air of Raeburn's crew, or the dragging nonchalance of Ellington's men.

The band doesn't get much contrast as far as dynamics goes—they play loud and fast as expected. Ballad singer Johnny Hartman provided a welcome respite, singing such near-dogs as *Lillette, It's Magic*, and *Old Man River* with a beat that marks him as another audience- ensnaring singer.

Dizzy Hits Another Hi-Note

Chicago—Constant attraction for visiting, as well as local, jazzmen, is the Anita O'Day-Max Miller combination at the Hi-Note here. Dizzy Gillespie dropped in the night this photo was taken, and was welcomed by Hi-Note owner Marty Denenberg, left, Anita, and Max, right. Dizzy was appearing at the Blue Note at the time.

Sunday 22 May 1949

Dizzy Gillespie Orchestra close at the Blue Note in Chicago.

Saturday 28 May 1949

Dizzy Gillespie Orchestra play a one-nighter at Laurel Gardens in Newark, New Jersey.

Bop's Dizzy:

Meaning, of course, the inimitable Dizzy Gillespie who returns to New York for the first time in five months when he headlines the Apollo Theatre starting June 3. Featured with his band are vocalist Johnny Hartman and Joe Carroll, bop singer extra-ordinary. Following the Apollo he moves to Phil's Click Club for a two- weeker on June 17th, and starts a long run at Bop City July 7.

Friday 3 June 1949

Dizzy Gillespie Orchestra open a one-week engagement at the Apollo Theatre in New York City. Also on the bill are Savannah Churchill and the King Odum 4.

Thursday 9 June 1949

Dizzy Gillespie Orchestra close at the Apollo Theatre in New York City.

Friday 17 June 1949

Dizzy Gillespie Orchestra open a two-week engagement at the Click Club in Philadelphia.

Thursday 30 June 1949

Dizzy Gillespie Orchestra close at the Click Club in Philadelphia.

Friday 1 July 1949

Down Beat reviews Dizzy's latest Victor release:

Dizzy Gillespie
** *Swedish Suite*
** *I Should Care*

Gillespie playing the blues as modified by bop and an Afro-Cuban rhythm section. The arrangement, horror of horrors, inserts a cycle of fifths which the boys repeat in figures. The playing is lugubrious and not very conducive to heated reaction on the listener's part. Diz' solo is technically apt, but sounds much like other things that have occurred in the night before. Perhaps fronting a big band is getting him down—it certainly seems to have limited the ideas he is using. There is certainly no excuse for the band fronted by one of the best known names in jazz sounding this mediocre. The intonation and the attack of all the sections is uniforly sloppy. Certainly manager Willard Alexander and Gillespie can do better than this. *Care* is warbled by Johnny Hartman. (**Victor 20-3457**)

Wednesday 6 July 1949

Dizzy Gillespie Orchestra record for Victor in New York City. J. J. Johnson joins the band.

DIZZY GILLESPIE, BENNY HARRIS, WILLIE COOK, ELMON WRIGHT (trumpets); J. J. JOHNSON, CHARLES GREENLEE, SAM HURT (trombones); JOHN BROWN, ERNIE HENRY (alto sax); JOE GAYLES, YUSEF LATEEF (tenor sax); AL GIBSON (baritone sax); JAMES FOREMAN JR (piano); AL McKIBBON (bass); TEDDY STEWART (drums); VINCE GUERRO (conga); JOE CARROLL (vocal)
Hey Pete (vJC, DG) / *Jumpin' With Symphony Sid* / *If Love Is Trouble* (vJH) / *In The Land Of Oo-Bla-Dee* (vDG, JC)

Thursday 7 July 1949

Dizzy Gillespie Orchestra open a four-week engagement at Bop City in New York City. Sharing the bill are Dinah Washington and The Ravens.

Monday 25 July 1949

Dizzy Gillespie is at LaGuardia Airport to say farewell to the Deep River Boys, who are flying to London to appear at the Royal Command Performance.

Shaw Says Dizzy Owes Him 17 Gees

New York—Milt Shaw, former personal manager of Dizzy Gillespie, is suing Dizzy for $17,300 which he claims is owed to him in commissions. Dizzy and Shaw split nine months ago.

Shaw says the $17,300 represents commissions due him both before and since the split. He also wants his seven-year contract with Dizzy to be fulfilled. Shaw says it still has four years to go.

Two Emerge From Conference Room

New York—Willard Alexander may be the Gentleman Agent and Dizzy Gillespie Mr. Bop himself, but they're just a couple of the boys, according to this photo. Willard and Dizzy have some plans on making the Gillespie band more salable, which are outlined in this issue.

Friday 29 July 1949

Down Beat reviews Dizzy Gillespie's latest Victor release:

Dizzy Gillespie
** *That Old Black Magic*
** *Jump Did-Le Ba*

Magic's opening sounds like a Cuban *Riders in the Sky*. However, by means of a bolero segue a little sloppily played, it comes back to the tune and a Johnny Hartman vocal. The score is most undistinguished. Even with commercial limitations, Gillespie, and a tune as good as this, you would expect more. *Le Ba* is no relation to the old New Orleans tune, but a duo vocal affair, with Joe Carroll getting off the vowels with alacrity. Bop singing, which originally was a vocal projection of instrumental ideas, has become just as commercial as the Calloway scat singing, which was a perversion of the Armstrong vocal jazz efforts. The band's playing still is generally messy, though the intonation does seem to be improving. Gillespie and his manager, Willard Alexander, are evidently looking for a music which will purvey bop commercially. My own meager opinion is that records such as these appeal neither to the limited audience that likes bop nor the general record buying public. It's the old story of sitting astride a picket fence and writing endorsements for banana companies. (**Victor 20-3481**)

Wednesday 3 August 1949

Dizzy Gillespie Orchestra close at Bop City in New York and with Dinah Washington and the Ravens go on to make a short package tour. It is during this tour that they are probably recorded for AFRS Jubilee shows 357 and 359.

Saturday 20 August 1949

Dizzy Gillespie Orchestra open a one-week engagement at Club 86 in Geneva, New York.

Cyclist Diz Bruised As Auto Clips Him

Geneva, N. Y.—Dizzy Gillespie nursed a badly skinned right forearm as the result of being hit by a car while he was riding a bicycle here recently. The accident also caused an impromptu reunion of band leaders.

The bop trumpeter, in his own words, "was riding along, minding my own business, when—Bop!—I was hit from behind and was flying 10 feet over the handlebars.

"The motorist stopped and helped me up. Then who should pull up in a car but Erskine Hawkins, on his way from Saginaw, Mich., to New York."

The injury was treated at Geneva General hospital.

Friday 26 August 1949

Dizzy Gillespie Orchestra close at Club 86 in Geneva, New York.

Dizzy Gillespie appears on the cover of *Down Beat*.

J.J. Leaves Diz

New York—J. J. Johnson has left Dizzy Gillespie's band. Matthew Gee, formerly with Erskine Hawkins, has taken his chair with the Diz.

Following changes were made by Dizzy Gillespie: Don Slaughter, trumpet, for Bennie Harris; Harnifin Mageed, trombone, for Andy Duryea; Rudy Williams, baritone, for Joe Gayles, and Jesse Powell, tenor, for Bill Evans.

Friday 9 September 1949

Down Beat features Charlie Parker who claims that bop is entirely separate and apart from jazz.

No Bop Roots In Jazz: Parker

By MICHAEL LEVIN and JOHN S. WILSON

DOWN BEAT

VOL. 16—NO. 17   CHICAGO, SEPTEMBER 9, 1949

Kaye Blasts Krupa For 'Insulting Biz'

Dinah Harks To Her Master's Voice

> GILLESPIE'S PLAYING HAS CHANGED FROM BEING STUCK IN FRONT OF A BIG BAND. ANYBODY'S DOES. HE'S A FINE MUSICIAN. THE LEOPARD COATS AND THE WILD HATS ARE JUST ANOTHER PART OF THE MANAGERS' ROUTINES TO MAKE HIM BOX OFFICE.

Saturday 24 September 1949

Dizzy Gillespie Orchestra play a dance at the Miramar Ballroom in Chicago. Bullmoose Jackson and his Band are also on the bill.

New All-American Trumpet Star

DIZZY GILLESPIE AND HIS ORCHESTRA

MIRAMAR BALLROOM

DIRECTLY FROM EUROPE

With His **15 Jazz Syncopators**
1. Piano
2. Vocalist
3. Trumpets

Plus

The Great Gillespie

Saturday Sept. 24

ONE NIGHT ONLY

Your Host

Dizzy Will Reopen Pittsburgh Nitery

Pittsburgh—The Carnival lounge, local mainstay for informal session moving into a new home, the old site of the Hollywood Show bar. New opening set for early October with Dizzy Gillespie's band doing the honors. Local gal singer Tiny Irvin will be with the Diz.

Early October 1949

Dizzy Gillespie Orchestra at Carnival Lounge in Pittsburgh.

Tuesday 4 October 1949

Dizzy Gillespie Orchestra play a concert at Jones Auditorium, Shorter Hall, Wilberforce University in Wilberforce, Ohio.

Dizzy responds to the Parker interview in *Down Beat's* October 7 issue:

Bird Wrong; Bop Must Get A Beat: Diz

New York—The Bird is wrong about the relationship of bop and jazz, says Dizzy Gillespie. "Bop is an interpretation of jazz," Diz told the *Beat*. "It's all part of the same thing." Last month Charlie Parker said that bop had no roots in jazz, was something entirely separate and apart from the older tradition (see *Down Beat*, Sept. 9) Parker identified the beat as the distinguishing factor of bop.

"It (bop) has no continuity of beat, no steady chug-chug," Parker said.

This lack of a steady beat, according to Dizzy, is what is wrong with bop today.

"Bop is part of jazz," Dizzy said, "and jazz music is to dance to. The trouble with bop as it's played now is that people can't dance to it. They don't hear those four beats. We'll never get bop across to a wide audience until they can dance to it. They're not particular about whether you're playing a flatted fifth or a ruptured 129th as long as they can dance."

The important characteristics of

people can understand where the beat is. We'll use a lot of things which are in the book now, but we'll cut them and splice them together again like you would a movie so as to leave out the variations in beat.

"I'm not turning my back on bop. My band has a distinctive sound and I want to keep that. But I want to make bop bigger, get it a wider audience. I think George Shearing is the greatest thing that's happened to bop in the past year. He's the only one who has helped it along. He plays bop so the average person can understand it.

"Anybody can dance to Shearing's music. By doing that, he has

made it easier for me and for everybody else who plays bop."

They Were Unhappy

Main pressure on Dizzy to make the switch has come from his wife, Lorraine, a former dancer, and his manager, Willard Alexander. For the last year, Lorraine has circulated in the audience on his one-niters, getting audience reaction and trying to impress him that a lot of his numbers were making the dancers unhappy.

From Alexander's point of view, the big hurdle with Dizzy's band, as it was, was scarcity of places where a big band which didn't draw dancers could be booked.

"We can't play small places that hold 100 or 200 persons," Dizzy pointed out. "We're playing big auditoriums that hold a couple of thousand, and you can't rely on the extremists to support you there."

Alexander says he isn't asking
(Modulate to Page 12)

> WE'LL NEVER GET BOP ACROSS TO A WIDE AUDIENCE UNTIL THEY CAN DANCE TO IT. THEY'RE NOT PARTICULAR WHETHER YOU'RE PLAYING A FLATTED FIFTH OR A RUPTURED 129TH AS LONG AS THEY CAN DANCE.

Friday 7 October 1949

Dizzy Gillespie Orchestra open a one-week engagement at the Earle Theatre in Philadelphia. Also on the bill are the Ravens and Dinah Washington.

Thursday 13 October 1949

Dizzy Gillespie Orchestra close at the Earle Theatre in Philadelphia.

Philly Enjoys An All-Star Bill Seldom Seen On Stage

PHILADELPHIA—Staid patrons of this city's Earle theatre, rubbed their eyes in amazement last Friday afternoon as an over-exuberant audience of bop and swing fans cast aside all restraint to sing, dance and generally make merry in the aisle. The all-star bill featured four super-units. The melodic melange of the Ravens quartet, Dinah Washington, Dizzy Gillespie's band and the Chocolateers was the combination that "moved" the audience to their unprecedented display of enthusiasm.

The dancing-in-the-aisles reaction has happened in other cities, but the traditional restraint of Quakertown's reserve has maintained the tight discipline for which Philadelphia is renowned. The explosive routines of the comedy dance act provoked a fever pitch of excitement, and as Dinah swung out, the crowd enthused even more. It was Dizzy's exciting "Manteca" that snapped the last chains of restraint and the aisles in the theatre quickly became a seething mass of joyseekers and fun-makers. The more the ushers attempted to becalm them, the more they danced and sang. It wasn't until the Ravens had closed the show and the curtain had fallen, were the exasperated employees able to regain some semblance as order.

Needless to say, "an uproariously enjoyable good time was had by all."

Monday 17 October 1949

Dizzy Gillespie appears in a *Horizons in Jazz* concert (8.30pm) at Carnegie Hall in New York City. Also on the bill are George Shearing, Harry Belafonte, Jackie Paris, Dave Lambert.

Friday 21 October 1949

Dizzy Gillespie's 32nd birthday.

Settle Shaw-Diz Suit

New York—Suit brought by Milt Shaw against Dizzy Gillespie has been settled out of court for an undisclosed sum. Shaw, who was Dizzy's personal manager until the boppist moved from the Gale agency to Willard Alexander had claimed that Diz owed him some $5,000 in commissions and loans.

Diz To Wax On Cap Label

New York—Dizzy Gillespie has been released from his contract with Victor records and has moved his band over to the Capitol label. Switch was arranged by his manager, Willard Alexander. Dizzy's deal with Victor still had eight months to go.

Although Capitol is considerably more bop-minded than Victor, Gillespie's new label plans to fall in with Dizzy's plan to make his band more commercial than it has been in the past. Emphasis in his Capitol releases will be on definitely commercial sides, with only an occasional bop number to keep his bop followers happy.

Monday 21 November 1949

Dizzy Gillespie Orchestra record for Capitol in New York City.

DIZZY GILLESPIE, DON SLAUGHTER, WILLIE COOK, ELMON WRIGHT (trumpets); MATTHEW GEE, CHARLES GREENLEE, SAM HURT (trombones); JIMMY HEATH, JOHN COLTRANE (alto sax); JESSE POWELL, PAUL GONSALVES (tenor sax); AL GIBSON (baritone sax); JOHN ACEA (piano); JOHN COLLINS (guitar); AL MCKIBBON (bass); SPECS WRIGHT (drums); TINY IRVIN (vocal)
Say When / Tally Ho / You Stole My Wife (vDG) / *I Can't Remember* (vTI)

Carnegie Hall
Mon., Oct. 17th
At 8:30 P. M.
Tickets on Sale—Box Office
$2.40-$3.00-$2.40

Horizons in Jazz

A Modern Jazz Concert Presented by Jimmy Diaz and Larry Robinson

Dizzy Gillespie And Orchestra With George Shearing And His Quintet

Featured Artists

Shearing Makes Concert Bow

New York—George Shearing made his New York concert bow with his quintet at a Carnegie hall bash in mid-October which also offered most of the other available musicians in town. Concert, called *Horizons in Jazz*, was the first jazz effort of promoters Jimmy Diaz and Larry Robinson. Their inexperience showed in the programming, i.e. the melange of performers on-stage and the marathon length of the program which finally broke up a couple of minutes after midnight.

Along with Shearing's group, *Horizons* trotted out Dizzy Gillespie's band, Harry Belafonte, Davey Lambert, and Jackie Paris, plus a combo made up of Al Haig, piano; Terry Gibbs, vibes; Mundell Lowe, guitar; Tommy Potter, bass, and Max Roach, drums.

Dizzy Improved

The band that Dizzy showed at this concert was a vast improvement over the ragged group which played Bop City last summer. The sax section has a strong, rich sound and the brass has come to some agreement on what's being played. The whole crew is beginning to sound as though they know what they're doing and are interested in doing it.

Dizzy himself had nothing particular to offer aside from what struck me as a completely straight chorus of *Summertime*, interesting for its straightness considering the source. However, a very learned musicologist informed me that he was playing double vibrato on this chorus. Could be, but if he was he might as well save himself the exercise because it comes out sounding as straight as a new pencil.

New Vocalist

Diz also unveiled his new vocalist, Tiny Irwin, in a couple of ballads. She has a reasonably robust, straightforward voice, pleasant to hear in an era when too many singers are attempting to outweird each other. The gal isn't too strong on personality yet, but that may come with time and confidence.

Friday 9 December 1949

Dizzy Gillespie Orchestra open a ten-day engagement at the Club Silhouette in Chicago.

Diz Sacrifices Spark To Get His 'Bop With Beat'

By PAT HARRIS

Reviewed at the Club Silhouette, Chicago
Trumpets: Don Slaughter, Willie Cook, and Elmon Wright.
Trombones: Harneefan Majeed, Sam Hurt, and Matthew Gee.
Reeds: Jesse Powell, tenor; John Coltrane and Jimmy Heath, altos; Paul Gonsalves, tenor, and Al Gibson, baritone.
Rhythm: John Acea, piano; Specs Wright, drums, and Al McKibbon, bass.
Vocals: Tiny Irvin and Joe Carroll.
Dizzy Gillespie—Leader and trumpet.

Chicago—To get his "bop with a beat" and to make his band the danceable combination he wants, Dizzy Gillespie has sacrificed some of the spark traditionally accruing to the name and reputation of his music. It's been a spark that has been flickering feebly for quite a while, and on the whole the new Gillespie crew is an improvement over the sad unit he's been travelling around with recently. But the bright, hot light that was there is gone.

Only seven of the old bandsmen are left: Al McKibbon, Willie Cook, Elmon Wright, Sam Hurt, Harneefan Majeed, and Al Gibson, plus singer Joe Carroll. With the exception of McKibbon, none seems strong enough to do much toward forming a nucleus around which to build a band.

Saxes in Tune

For once, the saxes are in tune, and the fact that they don't do much more than standard sax sections are capable of doing is incidental.

Paul Gonsalves, tenorist formerly with Count basie, contributes some pretty horn from time to time, as does altoist Jimmy Heath. Trombones, with Matthew gee playing a baritone trombone (a large-belled valve instrument with no visual relation to either trombone or bass trombone), are probably the strongest section in the band, and sometimes give Dizzy's aggregation a Kentonish flavour, as on *Taboo*.

Although Gillespie played more (in quantity) than we've ever had the opportunity to observe before, the band did not seem to be as lost when he moved out of the number as did the former outfit. Drummer Wright, described by Dizzy as more flexible than Teddy Stewart… keeps the beat Diz wants and somehow the band manages to swing. On such tunes as J.J. Johnson's *191*, it achieved a really exciting punch and drive.

No Clowning

Dizzy's trumpet, on occasion, is almost so subdued and pretty to be colorless, and reflects the general sound of the band from the sax section back to the trumpets. The Silhouette stage had only about 18 inches of space in front of the band for the microphone and singers, which might have been one reason Dizzy played so steadily. There just wasn't any room to clown.

Tiny Irwin, a Pittsburgh girl who has been with Gillespie since August, did her best job on a tearful ballad called *I Can't Remember*, which the band recorded for Capitol recently. She has some annoying habits of phrasing and enunciation which sometimes tend toward stridency. Joe Carroll, of course, keeps on in the same syllabic groove, perhaps the only unchangeable thing in the band.

Sunday 11 December 1949

Elmon Wright (trumpeter in Dizzy's Band) becomes a father when his wife gives birth to a son, Jerald Ernest, in New York.

Thursday 15 December 1949

Birdland opens on Broadway in New York City.

Sunday 18 December 1949

Dizzy Gillespie Orchestra close at the Club Silhouette in Chicago.

Friday 23 December 1949

Dizzy Gillespie Orchestra open a one-week engagement at the Apollo Theatre in New York City. Also on the bill are Moke & Poke, the 3 Poms, Pigmeat Markham and The Orioles.

Above: Part of the Dizzy Gillespie saxophone section at the Apollo. L to r: John Coltrane, Jimmy Heath (altos), Paul Gonsalves (tenor).

Thursday 29 December 1949

Dizzy Gillespie Orchestra close at the Apollo Theatre in New York City.

Monday 9 January 1950

Dizzy Gillespie Orchestra record for Capitol in New York City.

DIZZY GILLESPIE, DON SLAUGHTER, WILLIE COOK, ELMON WRIGHT (trumpets); MATTHEW GEE, CHARLES GREENLEE, SAM HURT (trombones); JIMMY HEATH, JOHN COLTRANE (alto sax); JESSE POWELL, PAUL GONSALVES (tenor sax); AL GIBSON (baritone sax); JOHN ACEA (piano); FLOYD SMITH (guitar); AL MCKIBBON (bass); SPECS WRIGHT (drums); CARLOS DUCHESNE (conga); FRANCISCO POZO (bongo); JOE CARROLL (vocal)

Coast To Coast / Carambola / Oo-La-La (vJC) */ Honeysuckle Rose* (vJC)

Tuesday 10 January 1950

Dizzy Gillespie records with the Metronome All-Stars in New York City.

DIZZY GILLESPIE (trumpet); KAI WINDING (trombone); BUDDY DE FRANCO (clarinet); LEE KONITZ (alto sax); STAN GETZ (tenor sax); SERGE CHALOFF (baritone sax); LENNIE TRISTANO (piano); BILLY BAUER (guitar); EDDIE SAFRANSKI (bass); MAX ROACH (drums)

Double Date / No Figs

Friday 13 January 1950

Dizzy Gillespie Orchestra open a one-week engagement at the Paradise Theatre in Detroit. Charlie Brown is also on the bill.

Thursday 19 January 1950

Dizzy Gillespie Orchestra close at the Paradise Theatre in Detroit.

Friday 20 January 1950

Dizzy Gillespie Orchestra open a one-week engagement at the Riverside Theatre in Milwaukee.

Thursday 26 January 1950

Dizzy Gillespie Orchestra close at the Riverside Theatre in Milwaukee.

Thursday 2 February 1950

Dizzy Gillespie Orchestra open a four-week engagement at Bop City in New York City. Diz is substituting for the ailing Louis Jordan. Oscar Peterson and Flip Phillips are also on the bill.

Bop singer Buddy Stewart (27) is killed in an automobile accident in New Mexico.

Monday 6 February 1950

Dizzy Gillespie Orchestra appear at a benefit for Buddy Stewart at Birdland in New York City.

Below: Bird & Diz at the Birdland benefit for Buddy Stewart. Tommy Potter is the bassist and 23-year-old John Coltrane is at far right.

Friday 10 February 1950

Down Beat reviews Dizzy's latest Capitol release:

Dizzy Gillespie
** *Say When*
* *You Stole My Wife*

Believe it or not, the basie band does a better job of imitating a big band playing bop than does Gillespie on these sides, This is really pathetic stuff when you reflect back to the rough but interesting sides Gillespie made for Musicraft and his first few Victor sides. *Wife* is a straight novelty except for a commonplace Gillespie solo. *When* is a Jimmy Mundy score, sounding like dozens of basie sides in the last two years. If Gillespie's band can't make better sides than this, both musically and commercially, it doesn't stand a chance in today's band business. There is no excuse for trombones voiced over reeds sounding as ragged as Dizzy's do on *When*. (**Capitol 797**)

Thursday 16 February 1950

Mel Tormé joins Dizzy on the bill at Bop City, replacing Flip Phillips.

Wednesday 1 March 1950

Dizzy Gillespie Orchestra close at Bop City in New York.

Friday 17 March 1950

Dizzy Gillespie Orchestra open a one-week engagement at the Howard Theatre in Washington, D.C.

Thursday 23 March 1950

Dizzy Gillespie Orchestra close at the Howard Theatre in Washington, D.C.

Nell Lutcher, Diz Gillespie Open At Apollo This Friday

In the parlance of show business, a two-for-one show popularly means two shows for the price of one, and from whcre we sit it looks as though the Apollo is inaugurating something new … a six for one show, or something. Seriously seems hard to believe that the show beginning on Friday, March 24th is beatable. A first run picture (and a terrific one) on screen; a wonderful group of talented stars on stage.

The picture first … because it represents another success on the Apollo's part in procuring first run pix … Humphrey Bogart's newest, and in many ways, his most exciting film feature. It's titled "Chain Lightning." It's the story of the new fighter-jet planes and moves along about as fast as those mighty new demons of the air. The love interest is played by lovely Eleanor Parker … splitting the interest that is between herself and those new sleek planes. It's a rousing thriller in the real Bogart manner, recalling past glories like "Casablanca," "The Treasure of Sierra Madre" and other Bogart greats.

But reasons number two, three and four all group together on the stage. For, holding forth after too long an absence will be the unique swing style of that "Real Gone Gal" Nellie Lutcher whose hit record tunes still manage to climb to the top of the lists. "Fine Brown Frame," "Real Gone," "Cool Water" and others have become almost classics in the jazz department and that infectious Lutcher style of singing just goes on and on.

Star number two … the man with the trumpet … the big glasses and of course, the infectious personality … Dizzy Gillespie and his crew of great musicians. Hear his new record "Carabola" … it's a honey! But whether you have or haven't you'll hear it at the APOLLO next week. And that's not all … for the cast is really huge.

Dynamic young Johnny Hartman, now out on his own after several years with Dizzy elected to come along with his former boss while breaking in as a single at the Apollo. Teddy Hale, the bop singing of Joe "Be Bop" Carroll, the fancy skating of Virgie and Elroe, and once again after a considerable absence, the comedy of "Spider Bruce" and his gang of laugh getters.

Friday 24 March 1950

Dizzy Gillespie Orchestra open a one-week engagement at the Apollo Theatre in New York City. Also starring on the bill is Nellie Lutcher. Johnny hartman begins his solo career on the same bill,

Thursday 30 March 1950

Dizzy Gillespie Orchestra close at the Apollo Theatre in New York City.

Friday 21 April 1950

Down Beat reviews Dizzy's latest Capitol release:

Dizzy Gillespie
* *Honeysuckle Rose*
** *Carambola*

Well, Dizzy has certainly travelled the circle: he now has a record radio-banned because of out-of-taste lyrics. There are vague indications of pandering which should go great in the juke boxes—certainly builds Dizzy's reputation as a leader. *Carambola* is credited to Heitor Villa-Lobos, the great Brazilian composer. As played here, it doesn't come off as too much, perhaps nobody has yet made a record on which you could see hip-shaking and leopard jackets. (**Capitol 892**)

Friday 5 May 1950
Dizzy Gillespie Orchestra open a ten day engagement at Club Silhouette in Chicago.

The band gets great reviews with *Down Beat* correspondent Jack Tracy noting: The sledgehammer effect of the brass section on a couple of the Buster Harding arrangements… The genuine, rocking Afro-Cuban beat on such things as *Carambola*… Girl trombonist Liston's melodic, pretty solos… The raw, but in-tune savageness of a couple of the show-stoppers… A Lewis piano solo on '*Round About Midnight*.

The personnel is: trumpets—Gillespie, Gerald Wilson, Willie Cook, and Elmon Wright; trombones—Sam Hurt, Melba Liston, and Matthew Gee; saxes—Jesse Powell, Jimmy Heath, John Coltrane, Paul Gonsalves, and Al Gibson; rhythm—John Lewis, piano; Al McKibbon, bass, and Specs Wright, drums. Vocals—Melvin Moore, Joe Carroll, and Gillespie.

Sunday 14 May 1950
Dizzy Gillespie Orchestra close at Club Silhouette in Chicago.

End of May 1950
Dizzy Gillespie Orchestra at Sunnie Wilson's Forest Club in Detroit.

IT JUST GASSES ME. I SURE WOULD HATE TO HAVE TO BREAK THIS BAND UP. MAYBE WE STILL CAN LINE UP THE FOREIGN TRIP WE'VE WANTED, AND STAY IN BUSINESS. BUT **I'M JUST NOT MAKING ANY MONEY** THE WAY THINGS ARE GOING NOW.

AT THIS POINT **I HAD NO BAND, NO RECORDING CONTRACT, AND NO DEFINITE PLANS FOR THE FUTURE…** FOR A LITTLE WHILE AT BIRDLAND, I PLAYED WITH CHARLIE PARKER IN FRONT OF A STRING SECTION… THEN HE'D DOUBLE UP AND PLAY A SET WITH ME IN FRONT OF THE RHYTHM SECTION.

Gillespie's Crew Great Again, But May Break Up

By JACK TRACY

Chicago—Dizzy Gillespie is in a dilemma. And it's a pretty ironic one. Until recently, he was fronting a not-too-valid excuse for a band. But it worked fairly regularly. Now he's got possibly the best band he's ever had, and it looks as if he'll be breaking it up any day. Because he can't get work.

The band came into the Silhouette here recently and few expected much from it. But the word soon got around that somehow Diz had made a great, swinging crew out of what had been just a month or two before a dispirited, out-of-tune shadow of the Gillespie band that once was.

Personnel Shifts

It may be due to the fact that Diz made three vital personnel changes. He added pianist John Lewis, trumpeter Gerald Wilson, and trombonist Melba Liston (Wilson's wife). They've made a vast difference, with Lewis especially, helping the rhythm section get a cohesiveness and drive it never before had.

And also adding to the renaissance is Diz himself. No longer do you hear cynical onlookers remarking that "Not only doesn't the band blow, but Dizzy isn't playing much any more, either." Because he is. Not only is he once again contributing fertile, imaginative solo work, marked by his staggering technique, but is playing lead trumpet occasionally, splitting the book with the rest of the section.

It's quite an experience to see Gillespie, neck bulging out even more than his cheeks, playing a lead that carries the whole band along by its sheer drive and controlled power.

Big Problem

But like we said, he's got a big problem. The band may be broken up by the time you read this despite the fact visiting musicians just sat shaking their heads in disbelief when they heard the crew. Practically the whole band Charlie Ventura band went out to hear Diz, then talked about it for the next week. Drummer Tiny Kahn play...

Gee; saxes—Jesse Powell, Jimmy Heath, John Coltrane, Paul Gonsalves, and Al Gibson; rhythm—John Lewis, piano; Al McKibbon, bass, and Specs Wright, drums. Vocals—Melvin Moore, Joe Carroll, and Gillespie.

DOWN BEAT

VOL. 17—No. 12   (Copyright, 1950, Down Beat, Inc.)   CHICAGO, JUNE 16, 1950

Chicago—Dizzy Gillespie may be blowing those runs and high ones with a combo pretty soon. At presstime he was trying to figure out how he could keep his big crew working. If no solution could be found, he was all set to call it a day with a big band. Sad thing is, the band when last caught was again a Gillespie band of old and was playing excitingly and cleanly.

Woody, Gastel Split Up; Still On Friendly Terms

Chicago—Woody Herman and his personal manager, Carlos Gastel, parted company early in May by mutual consent. Their association began late in 1948, after Gastel split up with another former client, Stan Kenton. Said Gastel by long distance telephone from the west coast: "It was strictly a matter of dollars and cents. I didn't feel that I was getting enough out of the operation to pay me for my time. We're still pals, however. Nobody is angry.

"I have personal obligations that prevent me from spending anything except for my payroll, current expenses of the band, and my own living costs," explained Woody on the phone from Washington, D. C.

Will Try Without

"Carlos is a charming gent, I am very fond of him personally, but I'm going to try to get along without a personal manager. GAC will continue to book the band."

Woody was referring, in part, to the terms of his release from his previous managers, Mike Vallon and Chubby Goldfarb, by which they collect commission on the band's income for at least another year.

Injunction Bars 802 Picketing At N.Y. Station

New York—Latest move in the running battle between radio station WINS and Local 802 is an injunction obtained by the station which bars the union from picketing or boycotting WINS from any point where a broadcast originates.

Scuffle started when WINS dropped its eight staff musicians and the union put pickets in front of the station, at Yankee stadium (WINS broadcasts all games), and in ...rants...

TD, Manager Split After Two Decades
New York — Tommy Dorsey...

Barnet Ork Now Up To 14 Pieces

June 1950
Dizzy Gillespie breaks up the big band.

Tuesday 6 June 1950
Dizzy Gillespie records with Charlie Parker for Mercury/Verve in New York City.
DIZZY GILLESPIE (trumpet); CHARLIE PARKER (alto sax); THELONIOUS MONK (piano); CURLEY RUSSELL (bass); BUDDY RICH (drums)
Bloomdido / An Oscar For Treadwell (2 takes) / *Mohawk* (2 takes) / *My Melancholy Baby* (3 takes) / *Leap Frog* (11 takes) / *Relaxing With Lee* (6 takes)

Friday 7 July 1950
Fats Navarro (26) dies.

Thursday 13 July 1950
Dizzy Gillespie attends the funeral service for Fats Navarro in Harlem.

Thursday 27 July 1950
Dizzy Gillespie opens a five-week engagement as a single at Birdland in New York City. They play opposite Charlie Parker & Strings and Coleman Hawkins.

Below: Charlie Parker and Dizzy on stage at Birdland during the July/August engagement.

Thursday 10 August 1950
Kai Winding replaces Coleman Hawkins at Birdland in New York City. Dizzy and Charlie Parker stay on.

Thursday 17 August 1950
The Lennie Tristano Quintet and Harry Belafonte replace Charlie Parker and Kai Winding on the bill at Birdland in New York City. Dizzy stays on.

Wednesday 30 August 1950
Dizzy Gillespie closes at Birdland in New York City.

Thursday 31 August 1950

Dizzy Gillespie and his Sextet open a one-week engagement at the Apollo Theatre in New York City. Billy Eckstine, the 3 Berry Brothers, China Doll & the Calypso Boys and Pigmeat Markham are also on the bill.

Wednesday 6 September 1950

Dizzy Gillespie and his Sextet close at the Apollo Theatre in New York City.

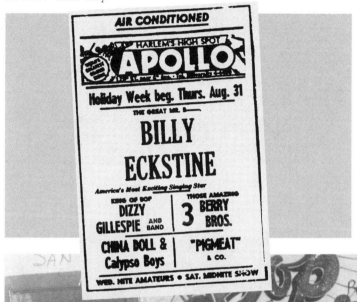

Dizzy is set to join the JATP Fall tour when some bookings materialize for his sextet Dizzy Gillespie (trumpet), Jimmy Heath (alto sax), John Coltrane (tenor sax), Milt Jackson (vibes/piano), Percy Heath (bass), Specs Wright (drums)

Tuesday 16 September 1950

Dizzy Gillespie and his Sextet record for Prestige in New York City.

DIZZY GILLESPIE (trumpet); JIMMY HEATH (alto sax); JIMMY OLIVER OR SELDON POWELL (tenor sax); MILT JACKSON (piano); PERCY HEATH (bass); JOE HARRIS (drums) UNKNOWN (vocal)

She's Gone Again (vDG) / *Nice Work If You Can Get It* / *Thinking Of You* / *Too Much Weight* (v)

Saturday 30 September 1950

Dizzy Gillespie and his Sextet open a two-week engagement at Ciro's in San Francisco.

Below: Dizzy and the sextet take part in a jam session at Jimbo's Bop City in San Francisco. Dizzy is at the piano with Miles Davis at his shoulder. Also visible are vocalist Betty Bennett, drummers Roy Porter and Specs Wright, Kenny Dorham, Sonny Criss, Milt Jackson, Carl Perkins and the Heath brothers, Jimmy and Percy.

SWINGIN' THE GOLDEN GATE

Dizzy Getting A Bad Deal From Music Biz: Gleason

By RALPH J. GLEASON

San Francisco—There is something radically wrong with the structure of a business which is not able to do more for its own true dizzard (Webster defines "dizzard" as a jester), John Birks Gillespie. Fifty has been anything but nifty for Diz and the fault is definitely not his. Here is a guy who really puts on a show. Who works. Who entertains. And, incidentally, *blows*.

And yet, the best they can do for him is a string of club dates, on actually a part-time basis, at a pretty low figure.

Ralph

Potentially, Dizzy is a standard name attraction in the music business. Musically, he himself is obviously able to take the first chair any time he wants to, and is a good enough band master to whip any crew of competent musicians into a good group.

From the standpoint of showmanship, he's one of the few modern leaders who realizes you have to do more than blow to get across to the public. And he does. He is a comedian—and a darned good one. As a buffoon, as a comic dancer, as just a riotously funny guy, Dizzy has a place.

Shouldn't Trouble

Add to this his marvelous ability to make musical sense and to *swing*, and there seems to be no reason under the sun why he should have trouble.

Once again, it seems to me, the fault lies with management. It's not just enough to line up dates (half the time that's a bookkeeping operation anyway), management should be able to mould an artist's act, to assist, to criticize, and to help him come up with something artistically valid—according to his own concepts—and at the same time something which will sell.

It's a question of presentation—sales-wise and publicity-wise. This is not being done with Diz. He's being sold as a bebop musician. He's so much more than the best connotation of that twisted word that it's a mortal shame.

Personnel

Diz' group consists of Specs Wright, drums; Percy Heath, bass; James (Little Bird) Heath, alto; John Coltrane, tenor, and Milt Jackson, vibes and piano. Specs (a fine drummer) and Coltrane are from Diz's last band. The Heath brothers are a couple of friends from Philly and good ones too. Jackson is marvelous and with Diz, who plays trumpet, piano and Cuban percussion, as well as singing, makes a great team.

Repertoire of the unit ranges from sheer comedy to great music and it always swings. Following their Hollywood Oasis stint, they are booked for one-niters in Nevada and points east on their way to the Silhouette, Chicago, there they go to Philly.

* * *

BAY AREA FOG: Tom the Crown Prince of Figs, to know if he's the only notice that Capitol's new singer Yma Sumac, is merely Amy scrutaned. He couldn't do with Xtabay, though, except Taxy. . . . Vido Musso in Black Hawk for two weeks October prior to Dave Brubeck turn. . . . Nick Esposo and Frances Lynne held over at Maurice Rocco did a week at Blue Angel in mid-October

Another One?

Fiddles Back Diz On New Releases

Hollywood — Playing footsies with fiddles has become a popular and lucrative pastime with jazz musicians lately, since Norman Granz started it all with the *Charlie Parker with Strings* album. Joe Bushkin followed, and now Dizzy Gillespie has entered the picture.

Discovery is releasing eight sides Diz recently cut on the west coast with a 23-piece band.

Featuring the usual string section, the group included oboes, flutes, and English horns as well. Conducted and arranged by Johnny Richards, the sides are mostly standards, with a few workings over of themes by Tchaikovsky and Rachmaninoff thrown in.

Discs are available on all three speeds.

Thursday 5 October 1950

Dizzy Gillespie and his Sextet close at Ciro's in San Francisco.

Friday 13 October 1950

Dizzy Gillespie and his Sextet open a two-week engagement at the Oasis in Los Angeles opposite the Lee Young Combo.

Saturday 21 October 1950

Dizzy Gillespie's 33rd birthday.

Friday 27 October 1950

Dizzy Gillespie and his Sextet close at the Oasis in Los Angeles.

Tuesday 31 October 1950

Dizzy Gillespie records with Johnny Richards' String Orchestra for Discovery in Los Angeles.
DIZZY GILLESPIE (trumpet); DICK KENNEY, HENRY COKER, HAROLD SMITH (trombones); JOHN GRAAS (french horn); PAUL SMITH (piano); JACK CASCALES (bass); SPECS WRIGHT (drums); VIDAL BOLADO (conga); plus harp, woodwinds and strings
Swing Low Sweet Chariot / Lullaby Of The Leaves / Million Dollar Baby / What Is There To Say?

Wednesday 1 November 1950

Dizzy Gillespie again records with Johnny Richards' String Orchestra for Discovery in Los Angeles.
DIZZY GILLESPIE (trumpet); DICK KENNEY, HENRY COKER, HAROLD SMITH (trombones); JOHN GRAAS (french horn); PAUL SMITH (piano); JACK CASCALES (bass); SPECS WRIGHT (drums); VIDAL BOLADO (conga); plus harp, woodwinds and strings
Alone Together / These Are The Things I Love / On The Alamo / Interlude In C

After the record sessions, the sextet plays one-nighters in Nevada on the way to the Silhouette Club in Chicago.

Friday 17 November 1950

Dizzy Gillespie and his Sextet open a three-week engagement at the Silhouette Club in Chicago.

Thursday 7 December 1950

Dizzy Gillespie and his Sextet close at the Silhouette Club in Chicago.

Monday 11 December 1950

Dizzy Gillespie and his Sextet open a one-week engagement at Club Harlem in Philadelphia.

Sunday 17 December 1950

Dizzy Gillespie and his Sextet close at Club Harlem in Philadelphia.

Monday 25 December 1950

Dizzy takes part in Symphony Sid's Third Annual Christmas Concert at Carnegie Hall in New York City.

Gillespie With Woodwinds, Etc., Plays Symphony Sid Concert

New York — Dizzy Gilles- | take out a similar unit on a con-
pie's "new sound," featuring | cert tour within the next couple
woodwinds, strings, trom- | of months.
bones, and rhythm, was set
for its first public appearance here
in Symphony Sid's third annual
Christmas jazz concert, scheduled
for the night of Dec. 25.

The Johnny Richards arrangements, recorded by Diz for Discovery, were to be played by an
orchestra under Ralph Burns,
Richards himself being unable to
come east for the occasion. A
Charlie Parker session with
strings was also expected to be
featured, with some of the same
musicians participating.

Diz, highly enthused by the first
reactions to the records, hopes to

DeVol Tops Gray's Palladium Reco

Hollywood—Fra
cently-organi
made its de
outdrew Jo
previous
several
the band
In hi
16,661
ing hi
the h
was

Jazz State Shocks Frenchman

New York — French pianist Jack Dieval, center above, discusses the limited audience given to modern jazz in New York nowadays with two men who were able to tell him a great deal about it. Dizzy Gillespie is on the left, and pianist Billy Taylor on the right. Dieval, who was surprised to find only Birdland giving modernists a steady billing, dropped down there last month to hear Dizzy's band, and that of Lester Young, who shared the stand.

1951

Thursday 4 January 1951
Dizzy Gillespie and his Sextet open at Birdland in New York City for a three-week engagement opposite Lester Young.

Saturday 6 January 1951
Dizzy Gillespie and his Sextet broadcast from Birdland in New York City.
DIZZY GILLESPIE (trumpet); JOHN COLTRANE (tenor sax); MILT JACKSON (vibes); BILLY TAYLOR (piano); PERCY HEATH (bass); ART BLAKEY (drums); JOE CARROLL (vocal); SYMPHONY SID TORIN (announcer)
Congo Blues / Yesterdays / Night In Tunisia / Oop-Pop-A-Da (vDG, JC) / *Jumpin' With Symphony Sid* (theme)

Thursday 11 January 1951
Dinah Washington joins Dizzy and Lester on the bill at Birdland in New York City.

Saturday 13 January 1951
Dizzy Gillespie and his Sextet broadcast from Birdland in New York City.
DIZZY GILLESPIE (trumpet); JOHN COLTRANE (tenor sax); MILT JACKSON (vibes); BILLY TAYLOR (piano); PERCY HEATH (bass); ART BLAKEY (drums); JOE CARROLL (vocal); SYMPHONY SID TORIN (announcer)
Good Groove / Tin Tin Deo / Birk's Works / Wow (vDG, JC) / *Good Bait / Jumpin' With Symphony Sid* (theme)

Saturday 20 January 1951
Dizzy Gillespie and his Sextet broadcast from Birdland in New York City.
DIZZY GILLESPIE (trumpet); JOHN COLTRANE (tenor sax); MILT JACKSON (vibes); BILLY TAYLOR (piano); PERCY HEATH (bass); ART BLAKEY (drums); JOE CARROLL (vocal); SYMPHONY SID TORIN (announcer)
Groovin' High / I Can't Get Started / Night In Tunisia / Oop-Pop-A-Da (vDG, JC) / *Jumpin' With Symphony Sid* (theme)

Thursday 25 January 1951
George Shearing's Quintet replaces Lester Young and Dinah Washington on the bill at Birdland in New York City. Dizzy and his band stay on for an extra two weeks.

Friday 26 January 1951
Jack Tracy, George Hoefer and Pat Harris of *Down Beat* review Dizzy's string album:

Dizzy Gillespie Plays,
Johnny Richards Conducts
Swing Low, Sweet Chariot
These Are the Things I Love
Alone Together
On the Alamo
Interlude in C
Lullaby of the Leaves
What is There to Say?
Million Dollar Baby

Album Rating: 5

Jack: This album of Diz with strings, woodwinds, etc., is probably going to sell more copies than any one single Diz ever made before. But it isn't that good. Sounds like jazzed-up Muzak, with only occasional flashes of fair Gillespie horn interjected. Seldom is the great sound he gets from his horn missing, but even more seldom does he combine it with his undisputed talent. *Million Dollar Baby, Alamo,* and *Chariot* are probably the best of the lot, with Diz even doing some singing on *Chariot* (and sounding as if he's having a great time). Album rating: 5

George: *Swing Low, Sweet Chariot* startles with a Dizzy vocal sounding not unlike Satchmo'. This side swings and moves between the two vocal choruses. The effectiveness of the bongo is offset by the ineffectiveness of the unison vocal.

The rest of the sides find Dizzy playing some fair horn along with some bad. The tunes are sometimes rendered prettily, other times there is a clash. Best sides are *Lullaby of the Leaves* and *On the Alamo*, which both have some fine piano. Album rating: 5

Pat: Generally innocuous work by Diz and a big band which sounds like an escapee from a movie soundtrack. With all those fine musicians and instruments at hand, it seems rather a shame to have used them in the way in which you will hear them on these sides. On most of the sides, especially *Baby*, Gillespie repeats Gillespie to a surprising degree. Best of the bunch is *Chariot*, in which the Diz' completely charming personality comes through in a short vocal and an unpretentious solo. His playing on *Lullaby* is also notable, but all in all, he should be encouraged to try this sort of thing again with better results expected. (**Discovery DL3013**) Album rating: 6

THE HOT BOX
Diz Starts Own Disc Firm To Wax What He Pleases
By GEORGE HOEFER

Chicago—No one suffered professionally more than Dizzy Gillespie as a result of the recent fiasco made of modern progressive jazz by the "Bop for the People" campaign indulged in by the Capitol and RCA record bigwigs. The type of tunes given Diz to record at Capitol were as ridiculous as giving PeeWee Hunt an assignment to wax *Groovin' High*. It's too bad Capitol's jazz consultant is hung on Kansas City's Vine street like a needle caught in a kick-back groove.

Nor did the Dizzy with strings experiment bring forth anything of note musically or, as was true in the case of Bird, a wider listening audience. Which all brings us to the current development, the Dee Gee record company.

Diz, Lennie Agree

Both Dizzy and Lennie Tristano have come to the conclusion that you have to do it yourself to come out with a result that is worthwhile musically and successful commercially. There is still a vague possibility that something that is good musically might sell enough to be considered a moderate success, or at least break even.

Dave Usher, a Detroiter who has been associated with Gillespie for some years, is handling the business end of Dee Gee records from the Motor city, and is Dizzy's partner in the enterprise.

The first Dee Gee date was held in Detroit last February 24, when Diz' group cut four sides using Milt Jackson, vibes; John Coltrane, tenor; Kenny Burrell, guitar; Percy Heath, bass; Kansas Fields, drums, and on one side the Calypso Boys, consisting of two bongo players and a wielder of the maracas. Freddie Strong did the vocals on a tune called *Love Me*.

Dedicated to Chano

Titles include a dedicatory number to the late Chano Pozo, written by the great bongoist in collaboration with Dizzy and Walter Fuller, called *Tin Tin Deo*. This was also recorded a year or so ago by James Moody with Pozo himself on Blue Note 555.

The reverse of the above on Dee Gee 3601 is a Dizzy original called *Birk's Works*, on which he is on a new kick of playing more in the middle register than has been his wont. A review of the two above sides will be found in the record section of this issue.

Not Yet Available

Dee Gee 3600 couples *I've Got the Boogie* and *The Be-bop* with

Love Me, a ballad appealer. record has not become availa for review as yet.

As usual with John Birks, has something startling on the fi The Dee Gee firm will also go for recording children's record and feature the Gillespie horn same.

JAZZ CONCERTS: The city Oshkosh, Wis., is going in f regular jazz concerts presented Carl Larsen and Benny Rhode They are called *Jazz at the*

Dizzy Gillespie and his partner Dave Usher, a long-time associate from Detroit, form their own recording label, Dee Gee.

Saturday 3 February 1951
Dizzy Gillespie and his Sextet broadcast from Birdland in New York City. Trombonist J. J. Johnson is added.
DIZZY GILLESPIE (trumpet); JOHN COLTRANE (tenor sax); J. J. JOHNSON (trombone); MILT JACKSON (vibes); BILLY TAYLOR (piano); PERCY HEATH (bass); ART BLAKEY (drums); JOE CARROLL (vocal); SYMPHONY SID TORIN (announcer)
Birk's Works / I Can't Get Started / Lady Be Good (vDG, JC / JJJ out) / *Good Bait* (vDG) / *Jumpin' With Symphony Sid* (vDG)

Wednesday 7 February 1951
Dizzy Gillespie and his Sextet close at Birdland in New York City.

Dizzy Takes Combo On New England Tour
New York—Dizzy Gillespie took his combo on a tour of New England following his date at Birdland. With him are Milt Jackson, vibes; John Coltrane, tenor; Percy Heath, bass; Ray Bryant, piano; and Art Blakey, drums. Willard Alexander doing the booking.

Friday 16 February 1951
Dizzy Gillespie and his Sextet open a ten-day engagement at Club Juana in Detroit.

Sunday 25 February 1951
Dizzy Gillespie and his Sextet close at Club Juana in Detroit.

Thursday 1 March 1951
Dizzy Gillespie and his Septet make their first recording for Dizzy's own label, DeeGee, in Detroit.
DIZZY GILLESPIE (trumpet); JOHN COLTRANE (tenor sax); MILT JACKSON (vibes/piano); KENNY BURRELL (guitar); PERCY HEATH (bass); KANSAS FIELDS (drums); FRED STRONG (vocal); THE CALYPSO BOYS (percussion)
We Love To Boogie (vFS) / *Tin Tin Deo* (vFS) / *Birk's Works* (percTCB) / *Love Me*

Thursday 8 March 1951
Dizzy Gillespie and his Sextet open a one-week engagement at the Seville Theatre in Montreal opposite Anita O'Day and Guy Mitchell.

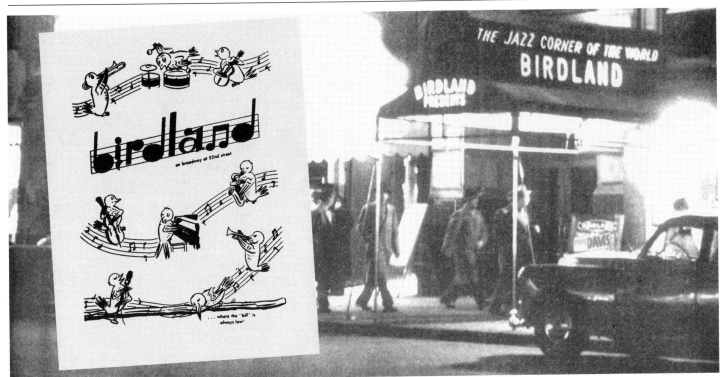

Wednesday 14 March 1951
Dizzy Gillespie and his Sextet close at the Seville Theatre in Montreal.

Thursday 15 March 1951
Dizzy Gillespie and his Septet open a one-week engagement at Birdland in New York City opposite Slim Gaillard and the Lester Young Quartet.

Saturday 17 March 1951
Dizzy Gillespie and his Septet broadcast from Birdland in New York City.
DIZZY GILLESPIE (trumpet); JOHN COLTRANE (tenor sax); J. J. JOHNSON (trombone); MILT JACKSON (vibes); JOHN LEWIS (piano); PERCY HEATH (bass); KANSAS FIELDS (drums); JOE CARROLL (vocal); SYMPHONY SID TORIN (announcer)
Birk's Works / Tin Tin Deo / Lady Be Good (vDG, JC) / *I Can't Get Started / The Champ / Jumpin' With Symphony Sid* (theme)

Wednesday 21 March 1951
Dizzy Gillespie and his Septet close at Birdland in New York City. Dizzy fires John Cpltrane, whose heroin addiction is becoming a problem.

Thursday 29 March 1951
Dizzy opens at Birdland with Charlie Parker in the band. Georgie Auld is also on the bill. Dizzy is to spend much of the next two months at Birdland both as a single and with his band.

Saturday 31 March 1951
Dizzy, Charlie Parker and the All Stars broadcast over station WJZ from Birdland in New York City.

DIZZY GILLESPIE (trumpet); CHARLIE PARKER (alto sax); BUD POWELL (piano); TOMMY POTTER (bass); ROY HAYNES (drums); JOE CARROLL (vocal); SYMPHONY SID TORIN (announcer)
Introduction / Blue'n'Boogie / Anthropology / Round About Midnight / Night In Tunisia / Jumpin' With Symphony Sid (theme)

Friday 6 April 1951
Dizzy Gillespie and his Sextet open a one-week engagement at the Apollo Theatre in New York City. Also on the bill are Sarah Vaughan, Eddie Heywood, Stump & Stumpy and Symphony Sid.

Thursday 12 April 1951

Dizzy Gillespie and his Sextet close at the Apollo Theatre in New York City.
Dizzy and his group continue at Birdland.

Saturday 14 April 1951

Dizzy Gillespie and his Sextet broadcast from Birdland in New York City.
DIZZY GILLESPIE (trumpet); BUDD JOHNSON (tenor sax); J. J. JOHNSON (trombone); MILT JACKSON (vibes/piano); PERCY HEATH (bass); ART BLAKEY (drums)
Good Bait / A Night In Tunisia / Birk's Works

Monday 16 April 1951

Dizzy Gillespie and his Sextet record for Dee Gee in New York City.
DIZZY GILLESPIE (trumpet); BUDD JOHNSON (tenor sax); J. J. JOHNSON (trombone); MILT JACKSON (vibes/piano); PERCY HEATH (bass); ART BLAKEY (drums); JOE CARROLL, MELVIN MOORE (vocal)
Lady Be Good (vJC) / *Love Me, Pretty Baby* (vMM) / *The Champ*

Saturday 21 April 1951

Dizzy Gillespie and his Septet broadcast from Birdland in New York City.
DIZZY GILLESPIE (trumpet); BUDD JOHNSON (tenor sax); J. J. JOHNSON (trombone); MILT JACKSON (vibes); JAMES FOREMAN (piano); PERCY HEATH (bass); ART BLAKEY (drums)
Klook [The Champ] / Congo Blues / Birk's Works / Jumpin' With Symphony Sid (theme)

Wednesday 25 April 1951

Dizzy Gillespie and his Septet close at Birdland in New York City.

Sunday 29 April 1951

Dizzy Gillespie and his Sextet open a one-week engagement at the Showboat in Philadelphia.

Saturday 5 May 1951

Dizzy Gillespie and his Sextet close at the Showboat in Philadelphia.

Friday 18 May 1951

Dizzy Gillespie and his Sextet open a one-week engagement at the Stage Door in Milwaukee.

Thursday 24 May 1951

Dizzy Gillespie and his Sextet close at the Stage Door in Milwaukee.

Friday 25 May 1951

Dizzy Gillespie and his Sextet open a three-week engagement at the Capitol Theatre in Chicago.
The sextet comprises: Milt Jackson (piano/vibes), Bill Graham (baritone sax), Percy Heath (bass), Al Jones (drums) and Joe Carroll (vocal)

Friday 1 June 1951

George Hoefer of *Down Beat* reviews Dizzy's first record release on his own label, Dee Gee:

Dizzy Gillespie

7 *Say When*
6 *You Stole My Wife*

Dizzy is on a new kick, playing a subdued, mellower horn more in the Miles Davis mode. It's a muted horn effect, using a large cloth (beret?) mute with squares cut out of it. On *Works*, the Diz still displays a terrific facility.

You will also hear bits by the fine vibes artist, Milt Jackson, Kenny Burrell's guitar, and some brush work from Kansas Fields, a jazz drummer of pre-war note who hasn't been heard from for a long time.

The second side is a tribute to the late Chano Pozo, who helped write this weird Afro-Cuban piece. Dizzy plays some mellow middle register horn backed by maracas and bongos. The sound is appealing, but not much happens improvisation-wise. A short bit by Milt is squeezed in. (**Dee Gee 3601**)

Thursday 14 June 1951

Dizzy Gillespie and his Sextet close at the Capitol Theatre in Chicago.

Saturday 23 June 1951

Dizzy Gillespie and his Sextet play a Jamboree at Reynolds Hall, Philadelphia. Earl Bostic and Joe Thomas are also featured.

Thursday 19 July 1951

Dizzy Gillespie and his Sextet open at Birdland in New York City for a two-week engagement opposite Dinah Washington and Slim Gaillard.

Thursday 2 August 1951

Lester Young and Oscar Peterson replace Dinah Washington and Slim Gaillard on the bill at Birdland in New York City. Dizzy and the band stay on.

Wednesday 8 August 1951

Dizzy and the band close at Birdland in New York City.

Friday 10 August 1951
Jack Tracy of *Down Beat* reviews of Dizzy's latest Dee Gee record release:

Dizzy Gillespie
7 *The Champ*
6 *Part II*
  Here's the first side that gives any idea of the excitement Diz can stir up in a club, where tunes like this usually run to 15 minutes or more in length.
  Men with Diz are J. J. Johnson, Budd Johnson, Milt Jackson, bassist Percy Heath, and Art Blakey.
  It's a romping blues, with Milt and Diz swinging away on the first side, proceeded by J. J. and Budd. The first three blow some grand things, but Budd gets hung up on a screaming jag *a la* Illinois.
  Unfortunate thing about the record is that it was split right after the first few bars of J. J.'s solo, so that deejays are going to have a tough time playing either side. That could have been eliminated, as the band repeats the original figure just before the trombonist comes in and makes an ideal spot for a break.
  Recording what he wants to on his own label is proving to be a boon for Diz. (**Dee Gee 3604**)

Thursday 16 August 1951
Dizzy Gillespie and his Sextet record for Dee Gee in New York City.
Dizzy Gillespie (trumpet); Bill Graham (alto sax/baritone sax); Milt Jackson (vibes/piano); Percy Heath (bass); Al Jones (drums); Joe Carroll, Melvin Moore (vocal)
In A Mess (vJC) / *School Days* (vDG, JC) / *Swing Low, Sweet Cadillac* (vDG) / *Bopsie's Blues* (vMM, 2 takes) / *I Couldn't Beat The Rap* (vMM)

Monday 27 August 1951
Dizzy Gillespie and his Sextet open a one-week engagement at the Showboat in Philadelphia.

Saturday 1 September 1951??
Dizzy Gillespie and his Sextet close at the Showboat in Philadelphia.

Monday 3 September 1951
Dizzy Gillespie and his Sextet open a one-week engagement at the Glass Bar in Edwardsville, Pennsylvania.

Saturday 8 September 1951
Dizzy Gillespie and his Sextet close at the Glass Bar in Edwardsville, Pennsylvania.

Monday 10 September 1951
Dizzy Gillespie and his Sextet open a one-week engagement at the Rendezvous Room of the Senator Hotel in Philadelphia opposite Meade Lux Lewis.

Saturday 15 September 1951
Dizzy Gillespie and his Sextet close at the Rendezvous Room of the Senator Hotel in Philadelphia.

Thursday 20 September 1951
Dizzy Gillespie and his Sextet open an eleven-day engagement at Birdland in New York City.

Sunday 30 September 1951
Dizzy Gillespie and his Sextet close at Birdland in New York City.

Wednesday 3 October 1951
Dizzy Gillespie and his Sextet open a four-week engagement at the Capitol Lounge in Chicago.

Saturday 6 October 1951
Dizzy Gillespie appears at an afternoon memorial session at the Gaffer's club to pay his respects to the late Jimmy Yancey who had died on Monday 17 September. Dizzy sits in with the Lee Collins Band.

Above: Dizzy Gillespie sits in with Lee Collins at the Jimmy Yancey memorial session. Among the bands which played were those of Jimmy Ille, Art Hodes, Lee Collins, Booker Washington, and the Royal Garden Seven (renamed the Chicago Night Hawks for the occasion). All proceeds went to Mama Yancey, the pianist's widow.

Sunday 21 October 1951
Dizzy Gillespie's 34th birthday.

Thursday 25 October 1951
Dizzy Gillespie and his Sextet record with Stuff Smith for Dee Gee in Chicago.
Dizzy Gillespie (trumpet); Bill Graham (alto sax/baritone sax); Stuff Smith (violin); Milt Jackson (vibes/piano/vocal); Percy Heath (bass); Al Jones (drums); Joe Carroll (vocal)
Caravan / *Nobody Knows The Trouble I've Seen* (vJC, SS out) / *The Bluest Blues* (SS out) / *On The Sunny Side Of The Street* (vJC, DG) / *Stardust* / *Time On My Hands* (vMJ)

Tuesday 30 October 1951
Dizzy Gillespie and his Sextet close at the Capitol Lounge in Chicago.

Basie, Holiday, Gillespie Head New Concert Unit

New York—A new concert package with a barrage of names rivalling the Ellington-Vaughan-Cole unit has been cooked up by Willard Alexander.

The unit, which will be known as "Carnival of Jazz," features Count Basie's full orchestra, Dizzy Gillespie's combo, Billie Holiday, and Buddy Rich.

All these attractions will appear today (Nov. 16) at the Philadelphia Academy of Music, and will do a second concert on Sunday in Buffalo.

After this, the combine will break up while its members fulfill previous commitments. However, Alexander expects to reunite the "Carnival" for a full tour in late December or January.

Friday 16 November 1951
Dizzy Gillespie and his Sextet appear in a 'Carnival of Jazz' concert at the Philadelphia Academy of Music. Also featured are Billie Holiday, Buddy Rich, and Count Basie and his newly reformed Orchestra.

Sunday 18 November 1951
Dizzy Gillespie and his Sextet appear with the 'Carnival of Jazz' concert package in Buffalo, New York.

Thursday 22 November 1951
Dizzy Gillespie and his Sextet open a four-week engagement at Birdland in New York City.
Arnett Cobb's Combo plays opposite the sextet for the first week, followed by Cab Calloway's Big Band, James Moody's group and, finally, the Dave Brubeck Quartet.

Cab, Dizzy To Play Birdland

New York—Cab Calloway will play his first Manhattan location with the reorganized big band when he opens at Birdland Nov. 27. Alternating on the "birdstand" will be a combo led by the man who worked as a sideman for Cab a decade ago, one John Birks Gillespie.

Wednesday 26 December 1951
Dizzy Gillespie and his Sextet close at Birdland in New York City.

Dizzy To Wax Children's Discs

New York—Dave Usher of Dee Gee Records was in town last week to set up the most unusual recording project of the year—a series of children's records with Dizzy Gillespie as narrator.

Discs will use special material written for Diz by Charlie Caudle.

1952

1 January 1952
Dizzy is third in the trumpet section of the *Down Beat* poll to Maynard Ferguson and Miles Davis.

Friday 11 January 1952
Dizzy Gillespie and his Sextet open a one-week engagement at the Apollo Theatre in New York City. Also on the bill are the Cabineers and the Clark Brothers.

Thursday 17 January 1952
Dizzy Gillespie and his Sextet close at the Apollo Theatre in New York City.
In late January Dizzy and the Sextet play an engagement at the Skybar in Cleveland, Ohio.

Thursday 14 February 1952
Dizzy Gillespie and his Sextet open a one-week engagement at Birdland in New York City. Also on the bill are the Dave Brubeck Quartet and Wild Bill Davis.

Wednesday 20 February 1952
Dizzy Gillespie and his Sextet close at Birdland in New York City.

Friday 22 February 1952
Jack Tracy of *Down Beat* reviews of Dizzy's latest Dee Gee record release:

Dizzy Gillespie

8 *The Bluest Blues*
6 *I'm in a Mess*

You may recall an article in our last issue in which Leonard Feather cited Dizzy for "striking as happy compromise as one could wish between musical and commercial considerations."

The Bluest Blues is a perfect example of what he was talking about. Joe Carroll sings ingratiatingly while a rollicking, romping rhythm section (Milt Jackson, piano; Percy Heath, bass, and Al Jones, drums) kicks along behind him. Diz follows with a wailing, bluesy solo that fairly crackles, then it's Bill Graham's baritone. The side really gets a great feeling.

Joe is restrained and breathy on *Mess*, shows dubious intonation. Diz is heard briefly. Not up to the performance on *Bluest*. (**Dee Gee 3608**)

Diz Strikes Happy Compromise Between Jazz, Commercialism

New York—Dizzy Gillespie has become a standard favorite at Birdland. This is not remarkable, since the same thing might just as easily happen to Les Paul or, perish forbid, Maynard Ferguson. What is remarkable is that Diz has achieved this modest but consistent success by striking as happy a compromise as one could wish between musical and commercial considerations.

Dizzy's band is musical. In its best moments, playing charming riff tunes like *Birks Works*, it swings beautifully, lightly, and Diz has been blowing some of the finest horn we've heard from him in years. Milt Jackson's vibrant solo work and Bill Graham's baritone sax are potent assets, too.

Economy

Dizzy's band is economical. He gets so much out of this setup that you do a double-take when you're reminded it's only a quintet. There is no regular pianist. Jackson, Graham, and Diz himself all double on piano, and of course Diz adds many Cuban percussion sounds when required.

Dizzy's band is funny. Since jazz does not live in a vacuum but is part of the great field known as entertainment, we find nothing offensive about the fact that bop vocalist Joe Carroll is a great laugh-getter. While his singing seldom achieves the stature of Leo Watson, who was obviously his early idol, Joe's sense of humor blends perfectly with that of the leader.

Fun, Too

If you don't hear them too many times, Dizzy's announcements are funny, too. He dedicates *The Nearness of You* to the Lifebuoy company and sometimes opens a set by apologizing for being late—"the Ku Klux Klan was giving a benefit for the Jewish Welfare Society at the Harlem YMCA, so we're lucky to be here at all."

After all the headaches Dizzy went through with his big bands, it's nice to see him making it with this combo in several ways: he's making pretty good music and making pretty good money, and making a lot of customers happy too.

—Jen

Dizzy Signs With Atlantic

New York—Just before leaving for France, Dizzy Gillespie signed with Atlantic records and cut his first date for the label, using Joe Carroll and the small combo.

Dee Gee records, the company Dizzy founded last year, will remain active. Dave Usher of Detroit, Dizzy's partner in the venture, is in charge.

Above: Dizzy Gillespie and Charlie Parker receive their Down Beat plaques from Earl Wilson and Leonard Feather.

Dizzy Sails For France

New York—Dizzy Gillespie was due to sail for France March 11 aboard the Liberte, to open two weeks later at the International Jazz Salon in Paris.

Willard Alexander's office canceled several weeks of bookings at the last minute to make the trip possible. Tentative arrangements called for a three-week tour of France, though offers from Belgium, Holland, and Scandinavia made it quite possible that Diz would extend his visit by a few more weeks.

The trumpet star is making the trip alone. Meanwhile his combo, under the leadership of pianist-vibraharpist Milt Jackson and featuring bop vocalist Joe Carroll, is being booked without him.

Sunday 24 February 1952

Dizzy Gillespie and Charlie Parker appear on a TV programme on Channel 5, New York. They are presented with *Down Beat* plaques by Earl Wilson and Leonard Feather before playing a number with the resident pianist Dick Hyman.

DIZZY GILLESPIE (trumpet); CHARLIE PARKER (alto sax); DICK HYMAN (piano); SANDY BLOCK (bass); CHARLIE SMITH (drums)
Hot House

Friday 29 February 1952

Dizzy Gillespie and his Sextet record for Dee Gee in New York City.

DIZZY GILLESPIE (trumpet); BILL GRAHAM (alto sax/baritone sax); MILT JACKSON (vibes/piano); PERCY HEATH (bass); AL JONES (drums); JOE CARROLL (vocal)
Dizz's Tune / This Is Happiness (vJC) / *Groovin' The Nursery Rhymes* (vJC) / *Love Is Here To Stay* (vJC)

Saturday 1 March 1952

Dizzy Gillespie and his Sextet open a one-week engagement at Pep's in Philadelphia.

Sunday 9 March 1952

Dizzy Gillespie and his Sextet close at Pep's in Philadelphia.

Tuesday 11 March 1952

Dizzy sails from New York aboard the Liberté. His combo, under the leadership of Milt Jackson, is booked without him.